Cambridge Elements

Elements in Philosophy of Law
edited by
George Pavlakos
University of Glasgow
Gerald J. Postema
University of North Carolina at Chapel Hill
Kenneth M. Ehrenberg
University of Surrey

LAW'S LANGUAGE

Meaning and Normativity

Daniel Wodak
University of Pennsylvania

Shaftesbury Road, Cambridge CB2 8EA, United Kingdom

One Liberty Plaza, 20th Floor, New York, NY 10006, USA

477 Williamstown Road, Port Melbourne, VIC 3207, Australia

314–321, 3rd Floor, Plot 3, Splendor Forum, Jasola District Centre, New Delhi – 110025, India

103 Penang Road, #05–06/07, Visioncrest Commercial, Singapore 238467

Cambridge University Press is part of Cambridge University Press & Assessment, a department of the University of Cambridge.

We share the University's mission to contribute to society through the pursuit of education, learning and research at the highest international levels of excellence.

www.cambridge.org
Information on this title: www.cambridge.org/9781009711364
DOI: 10.1017/9781009122801

© Daniel Wodak 2025

This publication is in copyright. Subject to statutory exception and to the provisions of relevant collective licensing agreements, no reproduction of any part may take place without the written permission of Cambridge University Press & Assessment.

When citing this work, please include a reference to the DOI 10.1017/9781009122801

First published 2025

A catalogue record for this publication is available from the British Library

ISBN 978-1-009-71136-4 Hardback
ISBN 978-1-009-11407-3 Paperback
ISSN 2631-5815 (online)
ISSN 2631-5807 (print)

Cambridge University Press & Assessment has no responsibility for the persistence or accuracy of URLs for external or third-party internet websites referred to in this publication and does not guarantee that any content on such websites is, or will remain, accurate or appropriate.

For EU product safety concerns, contact us at Calle de José Abascal, 56, 1°, 28003 Madrid, Spain, or email eugpsr@cambridge.org

Law's Language

Meaning and Normativity

Elements in Philosophy of Law

DOI: 10.1017/9781009122801
First published online: October 2025

Daniel Wodak
University of Pennsylvania

Author for correspondence: Daniel Wodak, dwodak@sas.upenn.edu

Abstract: The language of law includes normative or prescriptive terms such as 'obligation' and 'permission'. How do we explain the meaning of prescriptive legal language? This has long been regarded as a problem for positivists, since at first glance their view suggests we can derive an *ought* – a legal obligation or right or permission – from descriptive social facts alone. This Element outlines what we should want from a semantics of prescriptive legal language, critically evaluates four leading semantic accounts, and argues that legal prescriptivity is not, in the end, a problem for positivists.

Keywords: legal normativity, legal obligation, legal positivism, is/ought gap, deontic modals

© Daniel Wodak 2025

ISBNs: 9781009711364 (HB), 9781009114073 (PB), 9781009122801 (OC)
ISSNs: 2631-5815 (online), 2631-5807 (print)

Contents

	Introduction	1
1	That's Just Semantics	5
2	From "Must" To "Obligated"	14
3	Is "Legal" Like "Kantian?"	20
4	Hooray for Law	28
5	Are Legal Duties Made Up?	44
6	Hume's Law and the Law	53
7	Conclusion	60
	References	61

Introduction

The place to begin, nobody doubts, is with the language that law-applying officials use. In explaining the law, they cannot but use the language of obligations, rights, permissions, powers, liabilities and so on. What they thereby claim – and they cannot say it without claiming it – is that the law imposes obligations, creates rights, grants permissions, confers powers, gives rise to liabilities, and so on. The question is: What do these claims amount to?

(John Gardner, "How Law Claims/What Law Claims," 133).

In 1789, in a letter to Jean-Baptiste Le Roy, Benjamin Franklin wrote: "Our new Constitution is now established, and has an appearance that promises permanency; but in this world nothing can be said to be certain, except death and taxes." To imagine a world without death requires the help of science fiction. But, as anarchists like to remind us, imagining a world without taxes does not. Taxes are legally imposed, and laws are artifacts. There was a time before the US Constitution was established. There was a time before any legal system was established. For our early human ancestors, death was certain, but taxes were unheard of. Laws are a curious feature of our world: To be law-governed was not inevitable, but came to seem as natural as mortality.

What, then, are laws? Two observations push toward a particular view. The first was already mentioned: laws are artifacts. Humans make laws—whether by custom, democratic decision, or authoritarian decree. The second is that humans seem adept at making bad laws. Sometimes laws are objectionable because of what they proscribe: in the US in the early 2000s, sodomy was illegal in 14 states. Sometimes laws are objectionable because of what they permit: in the US in the antebellum era, it was legally permitted to own persons as property. The view that these observations support is typically called legal positivism. While many disagree about its best formulation,[1] the basic idea is simple: Legal facts can be explained by social facts alone. By "legal facts," I mean facts like the following: in the US, sodomy is now legal and slavery is now illegal. By "social facts," I mean facts about humans' attitudes and actions, such as how the US Supreme Court justices voted on sodomy laws in *Lawrence v. Texas*, 539 U.S. 558 (2003).

Legal positivism is the dominant view in philosophy of law, but it is not the only view. One prominent consideration that makes many reject it is the observation that legal facts and social facts seem too different. Social facts are descriptive; they concern *how the world is*. But legal facts seem to concern *how the world legally ought to be*. This is what Joseph Raz (1999: 154–155)

---

[1] See e.g., Plunkett and Wodak (2022b).

called "the problem of the normativity of law," and it arises due to "the use of normative terms to describe the law." Consider an example:

(1) You have a legal obligation to pay taxes.

This sentence seems true; it seems as certain as death. Moreover, it seems to be a kind of legal fact that is central to legal theory. Talk of legal obligations—and rights, privileges, powers, and so on—forms "the core of legal discourse" (Perry 2023: 721), and is commonly understood to express the content of the law in force in a given jurisdiction.[2] But if (1) is true, it puts positivists in a bind, as the relevant fact seems normative or prescriptive, not descriptive. Syntactically, (1) looks similar to moral sentences like:

(2) You have a moral obligation to pay taxes.

If (2) is true, it seems that there are facts about the existence of moral obligations. Likewise, if (1) is true, it seems that there are facts about the existence of legal obligations. So (1) and (2) are both true *prescriptive* or *normative* sentences.

As I noted already, the language of law includes many normative terms besides "obligation." Similar sentences concern legal permissions, rights, powers, and immunities. I refer to all of this language as *legal prescriptivity*, as the problem posed in each case is the same. If legal positivists tell us that we can explain legal facts in terms of social facts alone, they tell us that we can explain facts about *how the world legally ought to be* in terms of facts about *how the world is*. Many regard this as a grave mistake.

Hence, the continued support for legal anti-positivism. Many disagree about its best formulation too,[3] but the basic idea behind the view is simple: Law is in some sense a *moral* enterprise. We cannot pull a normative rabbit out of a descriptive hat. Legal facts must, in some sense, depend on moral facts. To get legal *obligations*, we have to start with moral *obligations*, and ditto for permissions, rights, powers, and immunities. The prescriptive language of law is often thought to lend significant credence to this view.

My goal is not to offer a full survey of the positivism–anti-positivism debate.[4] Instead, it is to offer a survey of what I'm calling *the problem of prescriptivity*. Since prescriptive language permeates law, how should we understand the meaning of this language? What, in other words, is the meaning of "legal obligation" in sentences like (1)? And does its meaning shed any light on the prospects for positivism or anti-positivism?

---

[2] This position is widely held. See Hershovitz (2014) for discussion and a case for its abandonment.
[3] Cf. Finnis (2002) and Atiq (2025).   [4] I'll henceforth drop the "legal" in these monikers.

Here's the plan. In Section 1, I outline what we should want from an account of the meaning of prescriptive legal language, such as the use of "legal obligation" in sentences like (1). Then in Section 2, I outline a formal semantics for "legal obligation" in sentences like (1) based on the dominant ("Kratzerian") account of cognate terms in philosophy of language. These two sections are intended to provide a clear framework for the rest of the project.

In Section 3, I discuss the most dominant positivist account (from Joseph Raz, Scott Shapiro, Jules Coleman, and others). On this *moral perspectival view*, legal obligations are like Kantian obligations—they are moral obligations from the legal perspective, where the legal perspective is understood as a moral theory. So (1) roughly means "According to the legal perspective, you have a moral obligation to pay taxes." As such, "obligation" has a distinctively moral meaning in (1), but (1) can be true even when (2) is false. Each of the core commitments of moral perspectivalism generates serious problems. The commitment to a *moral* semantics creates problems with linguistic data and univocality, and the commitment to a *perspectival* semantics creates problems with embedding.

In Section 4, I discuss the next most influential positivist account (from H.L.A. Hart and Kevin Toh). This *expressivist view* holds that we explain the meaning of sentences like (1) via the attitudes that they express, and the relevant uses of sentences like (1) express the speaker's acceptance of legal norms. States of norm-acceptance are non-cognitive—they are like desires, not like beliefs—so they are not capable of being true or false. On this view, then, sentences like (1) turn out to be neither true nor false. This is a radical departure from Kratzerian view, and it faces significant challenges. In fact, this view struggles on every desideratum for a semantic theory: it is hard to generalize the view from "legal obligation" to "legal permission"; it cannot avoid positing lexical ambiguities without any supporting evidence; it struggles to explain the meaning of (1) when it is embedded (e.g., "If (1), then p"); it makes implausible predictions about linguistic data; and it is makes implausible claims about speakers' psychologies.

In Section 5, I discuss a final positivist view (drawing on work by Jeremy Bentham, Hans Kelsen, and others). This *fictionalist view* is in some respects similar to moral perspectivalism, as it takes sentences like (1) to be understood as concerning what obligations you have according to a perspective. But there are three key differences: the relevant perspective is a fiction, not a theory; the perspective concerns a generic rather than a moral meaning of "obligation"; and most crucially, the perspective does not feature in the literal meaning of (1), but rather in what's asserted by uttering (1). Fictionalism can thereby offer the most straightforward semantics for claims like (1); it sticks closely to a standard

Kratzerian view, but, I argue, has distinct advantages in legal philosophy. The main reason for this is as follows. Moral realists often understand (2) to be true when paying taxes is supported by moral reasons. The fictionalist can similarly say that (1) is true when paying taxes is supported by legal reasons. But the fictionalist says this without taking on any mysterious commitments; legal reasons, we can say, are nothing more than reasons that exist according to a legal fiction. This is the theoretical option that I find most attractive, and I provide a tentative case for it below.

In Section 6, I return to whether legal prescriptivity sheds light on positivism and anti-positivism. While the question of what "legal obligation" means is difficult, interesting, and important, I argue that it leaves the prospects for positivism (and anti-positivism) largely unscathed. This is partly because positivists have reasonable solutions to the problem of prescriptivity, but it is mainly because legal prescriptivity may be a pseudo-problem. Once we are careful in understanding the sense in which positivists get an *ought* from an *is* (i.e., explain legal obligations in terms of descriptive social facts), this move plausibly involves no grave logical, metaphysical, or epistemic error.

That's the agenda. Before we delve in, I'll note three main upshots for jurisprudence.

First, much of classical jurisprudence concerns or is explicitly about semantics, but the field has largely proceeded in isolation from the relevant literature in philosophy of language, ignoring both substantive views and standard methodological commitments. This is a serious mistake. Second, much of contemporary legal philosophy treats "legal obligation" as a shorthand for legal prescriptivity writ large. The underlying assumption seems to be that a view about "legal obligations" will straightforwardly generalize to "legal permissions," "legal rights," "legal powers," "legal immunities," and so on. But nothing is said to support that assumption. And as we shall see, even generalizing from "legal obligations" to "legal permissions" often proves challenging. Finally, this project concerns the language of law in talk of how it imposes obligations, creates rights, grants permissions, confers powers, gives rise to liabilities, and so on. But as such, the project is intimately connected to inquiry into the nature of law. Close attention to philosophy of language may reveal that a central preoccupation of the positivism–anti-positivism debate is a pseudo-problem; at the same time, this attention can make perspicuous neglected challenges for views about the metaphysics of law, or reveal further sources of support for certain commitments about the metaphysics of law. So, if you're not gripped by philosophical questions about the language of law and only care about its nature, my hope is that you will still find much of interest below.

1 That's Just Semantics

Here's a striking observation about the state of play in contemporary legal philosophy. A central, long-standing debate in the field concerns the meaning of terms like "legal obligation" in sentences like (1): "You have a legal obligation to pay taxes." Philosophers of language have made great progress in developing semantic theories, and in identifying the appropriate tools and resources we should use to evaluate such theories. Yet philosophers of law have, until recently, entirely ignored all of that work.

To illustrate the point, consider the following passage from Jules Coleman, a key defender of the *moral perspectival view*, which Coleman calls the *moral semantics claim*. Here is Coleman offering to "explain more precisely what the moral semantics claim is." Coleman's more precise explanation is that this semantic theory is "a claim about how the content of the law can be (accurately or truthfully) described" (2007: 592):

> In claiming that law calls for a moral semantics, the thought is as follows. 'Mail fraud is illegal' expresses the directive: 'mail fraud is not to be done.' That is the content of the law. The moral semantics claim is that 'mail fraud is not to be done' can be redescribed truthfully as 'mail fraud is morally wrong'.

Coleman develops this thought further by drawing on Donald Davidson's philosophy of action. Very briefly, we are to understand the meaning of a sentence by thinking about truthful redescriptions of the act of asserting that sentence.

The striking observation is that in seeking to "explain more precisely" a claim about semantics, a prominent philosopher of law appeals to philosophy of *action* rather than to philosophy of *language*. If the appeal had been to philosophy of language instead, the more precise explanation of the claim would be quite different. The orthodox approach to semantics in philosophy of language is aptly conveyed by the first sentence of Irene Heim and Angelika Kratzer's *Semantics in Generative Grammar*: "To know the meaning of a sentence is to know its truth-conditions" (1998: 1). This may sound similar, but it is completely different. After all, as John Austin (1975) famously observed, a single act of speaking can be truthfully redescribed in three different kinds of ways, only one of which relates to semantics: *The semantic or literal significance of the utterance.*

I'll briefly illustrate Austin's distinction and its importance for the present project with a standard example. Consider someone uttering "Is there any salt?" at the dinner table. The *locutionary act* is to ask a question about the presence of salt. The *illocutionary act* is to make a request, as in "Please give me some salt." The *perlocutionary act* will (hopefully) be to cause someone to pass the salt. That's Austin's trifold distinction. So which act captures the semantic or literal significance of the utterance? The locutionary act! To see why this matters, suppose we explained the literal meaning of the utterance in terms of the illocutionary act thereby performed. Now imagine a geologist who utters "Is there any salt?" while looking at a rock sample. Does this utterance also literally mean "Please give me some salt," such that the geologist is making a bizarre request? Or do we now need to posit that the literal meaning of "Is there any salt?" is ambiguous in these two contexts? Hopefully this is enough to convey why understanding an account of semantics in terms of speech acts can easily go astray unless great care is taken to isolate the locutionary act. Despite this, Coleman does not assert, or provide any support for, the view that the *locutionary*—as opposed to illocutionary or perlocutionary—act of uttering "Mail fraud is illegal" can be redescribed truthfully as the act of saying "Mail fraud is not to be done" or "Mail fraud is morally wrong."

How, then, would we test a claim about semantics, such as the view that "Mail fraud is illegal" literally means "Mail fraud is morally wrong?" In determining the literal significance of an utterance, truth-conditional semantics—like all formal semantics—is guided by the principle of compositionality: We can compute the meaning of an infinite array of novel sentences via the known meanings of their parts.[5] This gives rise to an array of important considerations for semantic theories, which I'll discuss below.

Before I do, I want to note that much of Kratzer's most influential work in semantics is specifically relevant to the semantics of "legal obligation." Compare (1) to:

(3) You must pay taxes.

(4) You can file for an extension before the tax deadline.

Here "must" and "can" are used as deontic modals to express claims about legal obligations and permissions. Kratzer's classic, "What 'Must' and 'Can' Can and Must Mean," includes several legal examples (see 1977: 334, 347–351), and it has been cited more than 1500 times. But as far as I can tell, it took *four decades* for Kratzer's work to be cited in any publication in philosophy of law on the semantics of "legal obligation."[6]

So, Coleman is not a total outlier.[7] Until recently, the norm for any work in philosophy of law that concerned the semantics of "legal obligation" and other

---

[5] Ironically enough, Davidson also made this point. "The work of a [semantic] theory is in relating the known truth conditions of each sentence to those aspects ('words') of the sentence that recur in other sentences, and can be assigned identical roles in other sentences" (quoted by Heim and Kratzer 1998: 2).

[6] See Plunkett and Shapiro (2017: 60), Wodak (2017, 2018), and Silk (2019).

[7] Granted, philosophers of law often take semantics to concern "truth-conditions." But the term is used ambiguously and thrown around haphazardly: see the discussion and references in (Toh 2005: 86, 107).

prescriptive terms was to ignore vast swathes of philosophy of language. This is not to say that philosophy of law has yielded no important ideas or insights about the meaning of sentences like (1). But it is to say that such ideas and insights have unfortunately been developed in isolation from two extremely relevant bodies of work. The first is the general considerations that guide semantic theorizing in philosophy of language, which I will set out in the remainder of this section. The second is the theory of the semantics of "legal obligation" from mainstream philosophy of language and linguistics, which is most associated with Kratzer's work on modals. I outline that theory in the next section.

Let's turn, then, to the general considerations that guide semantic theorizing. I will focus on outlining the five main considerations that will play a crucial role in evaluating the different semantic theories that we will consider in this project.

Scope

Suppose that we had a theory *only* of the meaning of "legal obligation" in sentences like (1). An obvious concern would be that the scope of this theory is too narrow. Semantic theories should aspire to account for a broader range of related linguistic phenomena.

This consideration is particularly germane when we recall that the language of law includes plenty of normative terms besides "obligation." Recall the epigraph from Gardner: "The place to begin, nobody doubts, is with the language that law-applying officials use. In explaining the law, they cannot but use the language of obligations, rights, permissions, powers, liabilities and so on." Law-applying officials cannot help but use all of this language because the content of law includes legal obligations, rights, permissions, powers, liabilities, and so on.[8] Positivists need to explain all of this. And if there is a problem with positivists deriving an "obligation" from an "is," there is a similar problem for positivists deriving a "right" from an "is."[9]

Unfortunately, many philosophers of law offer semantic theories of "legal obligation" without explaining how the theory is meant to generalize beyond this narrow scope. I will focus on this project on generalizing such theories to encompass sentences like:

(5) People are legally permitted to commit adultery.

---

[8] This was a major theme in Hart (2012).
[9] See Chilovi and Wodak (2021); and see §VI below.

This is for three reasons. First, we have a good starting point for how to understand (3) and (4). The deontic modals "must" and "can" express "obligated" and "permitted," respectively;[10] (5) could be restated as, e.g., "Legally speaking, people can commit adultery." So, in Section 2, we will use Kratzer's semantics for "must" and "can" to clarify the meaning of "obligated" and "permitted," respectively, in sentences like (1) and (5). Second, there is plausibly a close semantic relation between "legal obligation" and "legal permission," akin to the semantic relation between "must" and "can." If "A must φ" is true, then "A can ~φ" is false, and vice versa. To illustrate: if it is true that "You are legally obligated to pay taxes," then it is false that "You are legally permitted to not pay taxes"; and if it is true that "People are legally permitted to commit adultery," then it is false that "People are legally obligated not to commit adultery."[11] Third, many think we can explain "rights" and "powers" and so on in terms of "obligation" and "permission." To have a *power*, for example, is to be permitted to change someone's obligations.

Univocality

Is "obligation" univocal in moral and legal sentences? Recall (1) and (2): "You have a legal obligation to pay taxes" and "You have a moral obligation to pay taxes." The question here amounts to asking: Does "obligation" have the same meaning in these sentences? I think so. This is supported by applying the standard *conjunction reduction test* for univocality. I'll introduce it with a different example. Consider the sentences: "Pale colors are light"; "Feathers are light"; "Pale colors and feathers are light." The first two sentences contain a purportedly ambiguous term ("light"); the third sentence conjoins them using that term only once in a context that encourages both meanings. The third sentence should elicit a linguistic intuition of oddness, as "light" is being used with two different meanings simultaneously. That kind of oddness has a name: *zeugma*. Because the third sentence is zeugmatic, we should think that "light" is ambiguous.

We can now easily apply the same test to "obligation" in sentences like (1) and (2):

(6) You have a moral and legal obligation to pay taxes.

---

[10] This is true when "must" and "can" are *deontic* modals, but they are not always used as deontic modals.

[11] What I say here is compatible with, but weaker than, the dual schema for "must" and "can" that is often assumed. Elsewhere, I argue that the dual schema is plausible only as a substantive, rather than semantic, commitment about specific modals. See Streumer and Wodak (2021, 2023). The discussion of weak and strong permissions (§III) also indicates why the dual schema should be contentious.

We simply conjoined and reduced the two uses of "obligation." But there's no zeugma. I elsewhere argued that this test and others like it provide strong evidence for the univocality of "obligation."[12] This provides a constraint on a theory of the semantics of "legal obligation." If such a theory says "obligation" is ambiguous in sentences like (1) and (2), then it predicts that "obligation" is zeugmatic in (6), which is false. We can also construct similar examples using other terms to modify "obligation" and cognate terms (e.g., "There is both a grammatical and moral requirement to φ") that are not zeugmatic. So this constraint on a semantic theory should be construed quite broadly.

We can also provide a similar test for terms like "permission." Consider an example:

(7) People are legally, but not morally, permitted to commit adultery.

If "permitted" were ambiguous in relation to "legally" and "morally," then (7) should be zeugmatic. But it isn't. In both (6) and (7), we vary *legal* and *moral* uses of the same normative term to generate evidence that those normative terms are not ambiguous in these contexts. But there is also a parallel issue worth considering: Similar sentences with legal uses of *normative* or *non-normative* terms. Consider the two conjuncts of (8):

(8) Positivism is a theory of legal institutions and legal obligations.

Is "legal" univocal in each of the two conjuncts? Let's check!

(9) Positivism is a theory of legal institutions and obligations.

If "legal" is ambiguous when it modifies "obligation" and "institution," then its single use in (9) should be zeugmatic. But it isn't. This provides another consideration that bears on theories of the semantics of "legal obligation." If such theories say "legal" is ambiguous in its two uses in (8), they falsely predict that "legal" is zeugmatic in (9).[13]

How costly is it to deny that these terms are univocal? To some degree, it depends on what is affirmed instead. One view would be that "obligation" et al. are *homonyms*. Another view would be that "obligation" et al. are *polysemes*, which have distinct but related meanings. "Bank" is homonymous rather than polysemous because its distinct meanings (riverside; financial institution) are unrelated. Some may contend that the tests above provide evidence that settles that "obligation" et al. are not homonymous, but does

---

[12] See further Wodak (2017: 273; 2018: 792 ff). On tests for univocality, see Sennet (2021). For recent work on zeugma, see Liu (2024).
[13] See Currie (2020: 120–121) and Plunkett and Wodak (2022a: 20–21).

not settle whether these terms are univocal rather than polysemous. As such, the reader may wonder at various points below whether a view about the semantics of (1) that suggests that "obligation" et al. are not univocal is in such dire straits.

It's a fair question, but I won't consider specific versions of it in the sections below. Instead, I'll make three general points about this response now. The first is that if one makes this response on behalf of any view discussed below, one owes an account of why the relevant distinct meanings of "obligation" (etc.) are sufficiently related for the term to be polysemous. But typically, those who have denied that "obligation" (etc.) is univocal have held it to have multiple *unrelated* meanings.[14] Second, other considerations also count in favor of taking "obligation" to be univocal. We need a general explanation of the close semantic relation between "must" and "can," and between "obligation" and "permission," that was described above. Moreover, we use terms like "must" and "obligation" not just to "refer to duties," but to refer "to duties of different kinds," duties of "different people," and duties "at different times" (Kratzer 1977: 339). If such terms are ambiguous when used to refer to different kinds of duties, etc., then we must somehow "keep billions of different 'must's" (1977: 441). We are finite beings. It is implausible that we store so many meanings for "must."[15] Such concerns about our finite cognitive resources for storing and processing language are widely understood to apply to views that posit homonymy *and* polysemy.[16] The third is that those who have most forcefully challenged the orthodox view that *modals* are univocal have, given the concerns above, affirmed that *deontic modals* are univocal.[17]

Embedding

Philosophers of language have long emphasized that a semantic theory of the meaning of "obligation" needs to account for simple sentences, like (1), *and* semantically complex sentences. By complex sentences, I mean sentences where a bare claim like (1) is used with ordinary logic operators (and, or, not, if … then). I've already mentioned several examples involving conjunctions

---

[14] For example, Hart (1982: 159–160) suggests we should be cognitivists about the meaning of "moral obligation" and non-cognitivists about the meaning of "legal obligation."

[15] Silk expands: there are "prudential 'ought's, rational 'ought's, legal 'ought's, aesthetic 'ought's, and so on"; a consistent treatment of all such cases would posit that speakers have "a proliferation of 'ought' entries in their lexicons," and that position is both "profligate and unexplanatory" (2014: 2–3).

[16] See Falkum and Vincente (2015: 3) and Wodak (2018: 793–794).

[17] That is, Viebahn and Vetter (2016) argue that there are several meanings for "must," but they agree that there is only one meaning for the deontic "must"—which is all that's at issue here.

above, and cases of disjunction are similar.[18] So I will mainly focus on cases in which claims like (1) are embedded.

One simple way to embed a claim like (1) is through negation. Here's an example:

(10) There is no legal obligation to be a Good Samaritan.

A theory of the meaning of sentences like (1) should also explain what (1) means when it is negated, so it must explain the meaning of sentences like (10). Moreover, plenty of legal discourse includes the utterance of sentences like (10). So philosophers of law explaining the meaning of "legal obligation" need to explain the meaning of (10).

Adam Perry (2023: 718) also provides a more complex example:

(11) All and only persons over 18 have a legal right to vote.

(12) A has a legal right to vote.

(13) So, A is over 18.

Two things about the example make it a good test case for a theory of the meaning of sentences like (1). First, it is a "mixed argument": "Some steps are legal claims, some steps are not." Second, the "argument is valid" (Perry 2023: 718). So, a theory of the meaning of (1) better be able to explain these features of the argument in (11)–(13).

Linguistic Data

Many subfields of linguistics, including semantics, rely on intuitions in testing theories. Much can be said about how to understand intuitions as linguistic data,[19] and how to elicit probative linguistic intuitions, but the following remarks are fairly uncontentious.

In "On the Methodology of Semantic Fieldwork," Lisa Matthewson noted that in aiming to "establish facts about the meaning of utterances, and parts of utterances," semantic fieldwork intuitions are helpful data. But the relevant "semantic facts are often subtle" and "are almost never accessible by direct native-speaker intuitions" (2004: 370). As such, "a researcher interested in the semantic contribution of the English definite article *the* ... cannot ask a native speaker, 'What does *the* mean?'" (2004: 371). Instead, the researcher must "construct a range of example sentences" to generate "primary data involving

---

[18] Though cases of disjunction are also the basis for many famous arguments. See, e.g., Prior (1960).

[19] See Santana (2020) for a careful discussion of the non-evidential role of linguistic intuitions.

judgments about the felicity and truth of whole utterances," from which "the semanticist reasons backward to establish the precise contribution of *the*."

We want to know the semantic contribution of "obligation." But we cannot simply ask people the meaning of "obligation." Instead, our semantic fieldwork requires us to "construct a range of example sentences" that use this target word, and elicit intuitions about the acceptability (felicity and truth) of those sentences. The example sentences should be simple, and contextual information should be supplied where relevant. If we construct sentences where rival semantic theories issue different predictions, this will elicit probative data. A central desideratum for a semantic theory is that it better coheres with such "primary data." A theory that fails to do so is in dire straits.

Linguistic data can also concern more specific notions than acceptability. We discussed one above: zeugma. Another is intuitions about semantically anomalies. "Colorless green ideas sleep furiously" is a famous example. It is grammatical, but it is intuitively unacceptable because the only eligible meanings would need to be utterly bizarre. Semantically anomalous sentences are often marked with a hashtag. Now consider:

(14) # You have a legal moral obligation to pay taxes.

This sentence is, I venture, semantically anomalous. There are legal obligations and moral obligations, but there are no *legal moral* obligations. A theory of the meaning of "legal obligation" should explain intuitive data about sentences like (14).

Psychological Plausibility

One final consideration concerns the motivational plausibility of a semantic theory. This consideration stems from a central point made by Hart in *The Concept of Law*.[20] Hart notes that many theories of law—associated with Oliver Wendell Holmes and John Austin, among others—suggest that people are motivated to comply with the law solely to avoid sanctions. Hart was concerned that this defines "out of existence" what Hart called the "internal point of view": The point of view of one who accepts the law and uses it as a guide to conduct (2012: 89–91). The "external point of view," by contrast, is a catch-all term: it includes "a practical attitude toward the law that does not involve acceptance," such as those who follow the law solely to avoid sanctions, as well as the non-practical attitudes of someone who "simply wishes to describe how members of a group regard and respond to a set of rules and, perhaps, who wishes to make

---

[20] This issue plays a prominent role in jurisprudence, but I am open to the view that it receives too much attention, and weight, without a clear account of its relevance to debates about metaphysics or semantics.

predictions as well" (Shapiro 2006: 1159–1160). A semantics of "legal obligation" should avoid implausible commitments about the attitudes of those who take the internal or external point of view. I'll refer to this as the *psychological plausibility* of such theories.

This consideration is relevant because it is often noted that the internal and external points of view are expressed using the same language. Since Hart, it has been common for the same language—e.g., (1)—to be called an "internal" or "external" legal statement depending on speaker's corresponding point of view. For example:

> *Internal* legal statements are assertions of law. They are normative statements made from the point of view of an adherent of a legal system. *External* legal statements, on the other hand, are statements about particular laws or legal systems. They are descriptive statements made from the point of view of an observer (Toh 2011: 109)

Notice that *the exact same string of words* can be an internal or external legal statement. I can say (1) as an "assertion of law" or as a normative statement made from the point of view of an adherent of the legal system. I can say (1) as a descriptive statement of a legal observer, as an anarchist who hates the law, or as an advisor telling you how to avoid being audited. If a semantics for (1) suggests that one who says (1) must be an adherent of the legal system, it has implausible commitments about speakers' attitudes; and ditto if it suggests that one who says (1) must, say, only care about the law's sanctions.

I'm going to focus on these five factors, but they do not exhaust the considerations that bear on how we should evaluate semantic theories. As such, there are significant limitations on the current project. Among these is the fact that it solely concerns English. Clearly a theory of the meaning of "legal obligation" is less plausible if it is not applicable to (at very least) closely related Indo-European languages.[21] But I lack the expertise to do that analysis with any rigor. And cross-linguistic comparisons are just one of the important considerations that I will not discuss at all below.[22]

My hope, then, is to offer a survey of how philosophers of law approach the meaning of "legal obligation," and to show how the debate could become more theoretically sophisticated by drawing on tools from philosophy of language and linguistics. The hope is not to offer anything close to the final word on any of the theories we discuss. It is, instead, to catalyze a richer debate between these views and other unexplored alternatives about this critical issue in

---
[21] See Viebahn and Vetter (2016) on the cross-linguistic applicability of Kratzer's view.
[22] See also Matthewson (2016) for relevant evidence about children's competence with modal expressions.

philosophy of law, and to explore its (sometimes substantial, and sometimes overstated) ramifications for the plausibility of specific jurisprudential theories, including for positivism in general.

2 From "Must" To "Obligated"

Kratzer's "What 'Must' and 'Can' Can and Must Mean" starts, charmingly, with the sentence "You must and you can store must in a can." The sentence involves occurrences of "different words that happen to look the same. The must which you can store in a can has nothing to do with necessity, and the can you can store your must in has nothing to do with possibility" (1977: 337). The point of Kratzer's example is that there is clearly some ambiguity with "must" and "can." But when "must" *does* have something to do with necessity, and when "can" *does* have something to do with possibility—that is, when they are *modals*—Kratzer proposes that they are univocal.

That commitment entails a weaker, even less controversial thesis that is relevant here: that uses of "must" that have something to do with obligation, and uses of "can" that have something to do with permission, are univocal. That is, *deontic modals* are univocal. Kratzer's semantics for "must" and "can" nicely illustrate how this weaker commitment could be explained. So a good starting point for this project is to explain Kratzer's view, then show how it can be generalized to "legal obligation" and related expressions.

Here, then, is a somewhat rough and informal characterization of Kratzer's proposal,[23] adjusted to this purpose, and explained in relation to an easy example:

(15) Since you are operating a business in the state of Pennsylvania, according to Pennsylvania's state law, you must have a business license.

This sentence is true when you file for a business license in every possible world that is consistent with the relevant descriptive facts (you are operating a business in the state of Pennsylvania) and the demands of the relevant deontic standard (Pennsylvania's state law). So, is it true? That depends on the content of the deontic standard; (15) is true when the content of the deontic standard includes some proposition like "If you are operating a business in the state of Pennsylvania, then you have a business license." The reason that (15) is an easy example is that it makes two things explicit. One is the *modal base* (the propositions that describe the circumstances where the obligation is in force). The other is the *ordering source* (the demands of the relevant deontic standard).

---

[23] For a more sophisticated discussion, see e.g., Dowell (2024).

Both the modal base and the ordering source are often left implicit, as in:

(16) You must have a business license.

Suppose someone said (16) to you right now. Is what they say true? That depends on the *contextually salient* modal base and ordering source. If that sounds mysterious, consider how you might respond: "But I don't operate a business!" Or: "But no law says I need a license for my business!" Both responses are germane because they show that for you not to have a business license is consistent *either* with the descriptive propositions describing the circumstances *or* with the demands of the relevant standard.

Here's a slightly more technical way of explaining Kratzer's view in terms of *possible worlds*. Take the sentence "A must φ." There is a contextually salient modal base: A set of circumstances that is held fixed. It generates a set of possible worlds (all the worlds where the circumstances obtain). There is also a contextually salient ordering source: A set of demands of some standard, like morality. Each demand may or may not be satisfied in any given world. Based on how well the demands are satisfied in any given world, the ordering source ranks (i.e., orders) the set of possible worlds. A world is better ranked if the standard's demands are better satisfied. Then we look at the best-ranked worlds. "A must φ" is true when A φs in all the best-ranked worlds.[24]

To illustrate the view once more, consider (3): "You must pay taxes." There is a contextually salient modal base (you live in a certain jurisdiction, you earn a certain income) and ordering source (which, depending on features of the context, may be the demands of the law, or morality, or prudence). Take all the worlds that are consistent with your living in that jurisdiction, earning that income, and so on. Rank those worlds by how well the relevant set of demands is satisfied. Do you pay taxes in all of the best-ranked worlds? If so, the sentence is true; if not, the sentence is false.

Since Kratzer takes the deontic "must" to "refer to duties," it is easy to see how the same proposal can be adapted to talk of obligations, like (1) and (2). I want to emphasize two features of the resulting view. First, it takes "obligation" to have a *generic* meaning. The meaning of "A is obligated to φ" is that A φs in all of the best-ranked worlds. I say this is a *generic* meaning to contrast it with views (see Section 3) on which "obligation" always has a *moralized* meaning: e.g., that "A is obligated to φ" always means that A φs in all of the morally best-ranked worlds.

---

[24] I'm framing this in terms of the meaning of sentences, but the meaning of "must" is a function from contexts to contents. This is somewhat technical. See Wodak (2017, 2018) and Dowell (2024).

Second, adding "legal" or "moral" to "obligation" marks a distinct ordering source (Kratzer 1991: 646). In other words, the Kratzerian view "permits a wide variety of values" for the ordering source; depending on the context, the ordering source could be "the laws in some locality" or "the content of morality."[25] So modifying "obligation" with "legal" makes contextually salient one way of ranking the relevant possible worlds, while modifying "obligation" with "moral" makes another way contextually salient. These modifiers, then, play the exact same role.

Let's consider how this view fares with respect to the five desiderata outlined in Section 1.

Scope

Kratzer offers a general account of the semantics of modals. The difference between "A must φ" and "A can φ" tracks the difference between universal and existential quantification. With "A can φ," there is a contextually salient modal base that generates a set of possible worlds, and a contextually salient ordering source that ranks those worlds. "A can φ" is true when A φs in *some* of the best-ranked worlds. The reader can probably see how this view will explain the meaning of (4): "You can file for an extension before the tax deadline." This sentence is true when in some of the best-ranked worlds, you file for an extension before the tax deadline.

It is easy to see how to generalize this proposal for "can" to talk of permissions. Consider (7): "People are legally, but not morally, permitted to commit adultery." Here a single use of "permitted" is modified by "legally" and "morally." We can start by taking the set of worlds that are consistent with the contextually salient modal base (whatever it may be). This sentence is true when in *some* of those worlds that are best-ranked by the demands of the law, people commit adultery, and in *none* of the worlds that are best-ranked by the demands of morality, people commit adultery.

Notice that this proposal explains the close semantic relation between "must" and "can," and between "obligation" and "permission." If "People are legally permitted to commit adultery" is true, then "People are legally obligated not to commit adultery" is false. Why? Because "legally" marks an ordering source, and the first sentence says that in *some* of the worlds that are ranked best by that ordering source, people commit adultery. The second says that in *none* of the worlds that are ranked best by that ordering source, people commit adultery. Those sentences, then, are contradictory.

---

[25] Dowell (2024).

Univocality

A core feature of Kratzer's view is that deontic modals like "must" and "can" are univocal. Consider examples like (6): "You have a moral and legal obligation to pay taxes." A single use of "obligation" that is modified by "moral" and "legal" is not zeugmatic; it seems to have a clear meaning. The proposal above explains this neatly. Indeed, a notable feature of this proposal is that it allows "must," "can," and other closely related terms to be univocal when they are modified by *any* set of demands—be they aesthetic, prudential, rational, grammatical, and so on.

Similarly, the view does not predict that "legal" is ambiguous in a sentence like (9): "Positivism is a theory of legal institutions and obligations." Kratzer's view does not offer an account of the meaning of "moral" or "legal." Instead, it suggests a natural view about how these words modify the meaning of words like "obligation." Because "obligation" is relative to a contextually salient ordering source, the inclusion of modifiers like "legal" and "moral" makes a particular ordering source salient. This in no way suggests that "legal" or "moral" *always* marks an ordering source.

Embedding

Kratzer's view is widely thought to face no problem explaining uses of "must" and "can" in complex sentences involving logical operators. (Kratzer [1977], notably, discussed many legal examples involving "must" and negation.) So we should expect a similar view about "obligation" and "permission" to face no problem explaining the meaning of these words when they are conjoined, disjoined, negated, or embedded in conditional clauses. Indeed, we already walked through an example involving conjunction with the discussion of (7) above. I won't dwell on this issue further.

Linguistic Data

Kratzer's view about "must" and "can" is well-supported by linguistic data.[26] I think that we should be similarly confident that the same is true of a corresponding view about "obligation" and "permission." I've also illustrated why the view does not predict zeugma in sentences like (6), (7), or (9). But it is worth walking through why the explanation of the meaning of (6) predicts that (14) will be semantically anomalous. If I say "You have a legal and moral obligation to pay taxes," the use of "legal and moral" makes two ordering

---

[26] Notably, even Viebahn and Vetter (2016: 15) grant that the Kratzerian view can "accommodate" the linguistic data that constitutes one plank of their interesting challenge to the view.

sources salient. By contrast, "You have a legal moral obligation to pay taxes" makes a "legal moral" ordering source salient; only there is no such ordering source! The view makes similar predictions about other analogous cases. *Conjoining* modifiers (e.g., "grammatical and rational") in modifying words like "requirement" makes two distinct ordering sources salient; *stacking* modifiers ("grammatical rational"), by contrast, is semantically anomalous unless there is a single eligible ordering source.[27]

Psychological Plausibility

The Kratzerian view under consideration provides a semantics for "legal obligation" in sentences like (1). On its own, it is compatible with different positions about speaker's attitudes; it does not define out of existence either the internal or external point of view.

As we will see below, many philosophers of law take the meaning of (1) to differ depending on whether it is an *internal* or *external* statement (i.e., whether the speaker takes the internal or external point of view). Further, many such philosophers insist that internal and external statements involve a difference in the literal meaning of (1). The Kratzerian view, by contrast, instead provides a univocal semantics for (1). But it is still compatible with holding that the speaker's point of view can bear on the *non-literal* meaning of an utterance of (1). The meaning of an utterance is, after all, not all literal.

Here's an early illustrative example of such an argumentative move. Richard Holton (1998: 611) held that a judge who took the internal point of view and said "You are legally obligated" could have thereby "pragmatically *implicated* that she believes there is a moral obligation," but "that doesn't mean she thinks she has strictly and literally said that there is a moral obligation, or said anything that entails this." I doubt Holton's specific proposal about this implicature and how it is generated. But many have endorsed more plausible views about how uses of "must" and "obligation" generate implicatures of the speaker's practical

---

[27] This explanation is compressed. Wodak (2018) explains it at greater length. The key idea is that modifying "obligation" with "moral" or "prudential" or "legal" has a *weak pragmatic effect* in determining the relevant ordering source for a use of "obligation." Modifying "obligation" with "moral prudential" (or "legal moral," etc.) has *inconsistent weak pragmatic effects* since there is a moral ordering source and a prudential ordering source but no moral prudential ordering source. Since this is a pragmatic effect, we can try to resolve the inconsistency by locating an alternative non-bizarre meaning for "moral prudential obligation." With some such stacked modifiers, there is such an alternative. Compare "grammatical rational requirement" and "rational grammatical requirement." The former seems semantically anomalous for the reason explained here, but the latter does not: an available reading is that the relevant grammatical requirement is itself being evaluated as rational.

attitudes.[28] As such, Kratzer's view is at least compatible with holding that speakers can say (1) with a different psychological orientation toward the law, and thereby implicate different kinds of claims.

Taking Stock

Kratzer's approach is widely described as the "dominant," "canonical," "classical," and "textbook" semantics.[29] That does not mean that the view—especially the simple version sketched here—must be correct, let alone correct in every detail. But it provides a good starting point for this project. It illustrates how a theory of the meaning of "legal obligation" can be compositional: we start with a well-motivated account of the meaning of "obligation," which then suggests a natural account of how "legal" modifies its meaning, such that we can explain the meaning of sentences like (1) in terms of the meanings of their parts. And, more importantly, it illustrates how such a theory can meet the desiderata discussed in Section 1: It has a broad scope, accounts for the univocality of the relevant terms, explains the role of logical operators, fits with linguistic data, and is psychologically plausible with both the internal and external points of view.

It would seem, then, that philosophers of law providing accounts of the meaning of "legal obligation" would be well-advised to build upon these foundations, and only depart from Kratzer's view on the basis of careful, considered arguments. But that has not been how the literature has developed to date, which is, in a way, surprising.

In a related context, Brian Leiter (2011: 665–666) wrote:

> Legal philosophy has, unsurprisingly, always been hostage to its philosophical climate—jurisprudents are rarely, if ever, innovators in philosophy. They, instead, are the jurisprudential Owls of Minerva, bringing considered philosophical opinion in its maturity (sometimes, alas, on its death bed) to bear on theoretical questions that arise distinctively in the legal realm.

Kratzer's truth-conditional semantics is certainly mature. It has detractors, but hardly seems to be on its deathbed.[30] Surprisingly, though, it has not been brought to bear on a theoretical question that is centered in the positivism–anti-positivism debate. It may be fine for philosophers of

---

[28] See especially the discussion of quasi-expressivism in Finlay (2014) and in Finlay and Plunkett (2018). For an example of skepticism about the empirical bona fides of this project, see Dowell (2016, 2020).

[29] See Horty (2014: 424, fn. 2) and references therein. Dowell (2024) also calls it "the canonical semantics for deontic modal expressions."

[30] See Dowell (2024) for arguments for why the most sophisticated rivals to Kratzer's simpler approach all lack some of its key theoretical virtues.

law to march to the beat of a different drummer. They just need to offer views that are either *compatible with* or *superior to* a Kratzerian view about the semantics of "legal obligation." Unfortunately, they've mostly offered neither.

3 Is "Legal" Like "Kantian?"

The dominant view among positivists is championed especially by Raz, Shapiro, and Coleman. Hershovitz offers a nice summary of the view and its main motivations:

> [These positivists think that] law employs the same concept of obligation as morality, so that claims about a person's legal obligations are really claims about her moral obligations. But they think that these claims are qualified in an important way. To say that a person has a legal obligation is not to say that she has a moral obligation full stop. Rather, it is to say that she has a moral obligation *from the law's point of view*. On this sort of picture, when you talk about your legal obligations, you are talking about the moral obligations the law thinks you have, which is roughly akin to talking about the moral obligations your grandmother thinks you have. A claim about what obligations your grandmother thinks you have would be a descriptive claim, not a normative one. And the same is true of claims about legal obligations, according to positivists who hold this sort of view. ... [C]laims about legal obligations are, on this picture, quasi-normative; they appear to be normative, but they are not really.[31]

The analogy to what your grandmother thinks is a bit too rough. A more perspicuous analogy for understanding the view is to consider sentences like:

(17) You have a Kantian obligation not to lie.

The literal meaning of (17) is, roughly: According to the Kantian moral theory, you have such a moral obligation not to lie. *Moral perspectivalism* adopts a similar account of the semantics of "legal obligation": "obligation" has a distinctively moral meaning, and the contribution of "legal" is to mark a theoretical perspective about morality.

Now recall the earlier examples of (1) and (2): You have a legal obligation to pay taxes; and you have a moral obligation to pay taxes. For moral perspectivalists, the literal meaning of (1) is, roughly: According to the legal system's moral theory, you have a moral obligation to pay taxes. To assert (1), then, is to assert *that (2) is true according to a theoretical perspective*. That perspective can be wrong; as such, (1) does not entail (2).

---

[31] Hershovitz (2014: 1169, emphasis in original, internal citations omitted).

Raz is the most famous proponent of this view,[32] but tethers it to some contentious commitments.[33] Those are dropped in the version of the view offered by Shapiro.[34] A similar view is held by Coleman, as we saw above; like Shapiro, Coleman says that "[t]alk of 'the law's point of view' is a way of expressing [...] an underlying moral theory that is implicit in the existence of law" (2011: 22), making the analogy to "Kantian" apt. John Gardner (2012: 133) embraces a similar view: "when, according to law, there are obligations and rights and so on, law's claim is that these are moral obligations and rights and so on."[35] Leslie Green also endorses the view (2002: 519). I focus on Raz, Shapiro, and Coleman as they explicitly say the view is a semantic thesis. There are several arguments for this view, which I engage with elsewhere.[36] Here I want to focus on how we evaluate it according to the desiderata for semantic theories from Section 1.

Scope

Moral perspectivalism cannot merely be a theory of the meaning of "legal obligation" in sentences like (1). It must have a broad scope, extending to sentences like (5) and (7): "People are legally permitted to commit adultery"; "People are legally, but not morally, permitted to commit adultery." At first glance, this does not seem to pose a problem. For moral perspectivalists, the literal meaning of (5) is, roughly: According to the legal system's moral theory, people have a moral permission to commit adultery. The literal meaning of (7) adds that people are not morally permitted to commit adultery. This is not self-contradictory. To assert (7) is, on this view, akin to saying: "Utilitarianism says you are permitted to kill one person to save five; but you are not permitted to do so."

But moral perspectivalism faces a subtle challenge in extending to "legal permission." The reason stems from an inconsistency between two claims. First,

---

[32] Raz explains "the meaning of statements of legal duties" in terms of the law's claims that "legal obligations are real (moral) obligations arising out of the law" (2009: 278). See also Raz (1999: 175).

[33] Raz holds that sentences like (1) and (2) can have the same meaning and express the same proposition even though (1) has descriptive truth-conditions and (2) has normative truth-conditions, and hence denies that we individuate propositions by their truth-conditions. On these details, see Shapiro (2011: 422 fn. 23, 414–415 fn. 44) and see Plunkett and Shapiro on Raz's "innovative semantic theory" (2017: 59).

[34] Shapiro says the claim that one is legally obligated to perform some action "may be understood to mean that from the legal point of view one is (morally) obligated to perform that action," where the "legal point of view" is "the perspective of a certain normative theory" about morality (2011: 185–186).

[35] See Currie (2020: 121–125) on Gardner's many formulations of the claim.

[36] See Wodak (2018: 805–809) for critical discussion of the main arguments for the view.

proponents of the view say that the legal point of view is "not a complete account of morality" (Shapiro 2011: 186); it is instead an incomplete moral theory. In other words, it leaves gaps: Some acts are, from the legal point of view, neither morally forbidden nor morally permissible.

Second, at least in many legal systems, "everything not forbidden by law is permitted by law" (Gardner 2012: 34). It follows that at least many legal systems leave no gaps: any action is either legally forbidden or legally permitted. For example, if committing adultery is not legally forbidden, then committing adultery is legally permitted.

The inconsistency between these claims arises once we consider moral perspectivalism as a theory of "legal obligation" *and* "legally permitted," in sentences like (1) and (5). Take the sentence: "If an act is not legally forbidden, it is legally permitted." For moral perspectivalists, this literally means something like "According to the legal system's moral theory, if an act is not morally forbidden, it is morally permitted." Ditto for any other way of expressing the view that a given legal system has no gaps. Moral perspectivalists, then, either need to say that legal systems *do* leave gaps (if committing adultery is not legally forbidden, it does not follow that it is legally permitted) or that the law's moral theory *doesn't* leave gaps—which would make it an absurd theory!

Even if the legal point of view is an incomplete moral theory, it may be absurd for other reasons. It is hard to see how the theory will "satisfy the demands of rationality and coherence" (Coleman 2011: 22). Among the class of actions that rational and coherent moral theories would consider to be highly similar, some such actions will be legally prohibited while others will be legally permitted—due to moral constraints on justified enforcement, institutional indolence, or myriad other reasons. This will make a legal system's underlying moral theory substantively irrational and incoherent. If that seems too harsh, try to construct a rational, coherent moral theory such that in a given legal system, every act that is legally obligatory is morally obligatory and every act that is legally permissible is morally permissible.

The law's moral theory can also be *structurally* irrational and incoherent. For example, even if legal systems shouldn't generate conflicting legal obligations, they sometimes do so.[37] The law's moral theory, then, must countenance conflicting moral obligations. That is a highly controversial commitment for any moral theory. In standard deontic logic, conflicting obligations generate deontic explosion: If there are conflicting obligations, then everything is

---

[37] See e.g., Hart (1982: 325–327). The point here is compatible with the familiar view that a legal system *shouldn't* contain conflicting obligations. The point is that when a legal system *does* contain conflicting legal obligations, the legal point of view is a theory that posits conflicting moral obligations.

obligatory. (Likewise, in standard classical logic, contradictions generate explosion: everything follows from p and $\sim p$.) At the very least, the structural features of the law's underlying moral theory can make it deeply implausible.

Univocality

Moral perspectivalism holds that "obligation" is univocal in (1) and (2), and hence predicts that mixed sentences that use "moral and legal obligation" are not zeugmatic in sentences like (6). Indeed, as we saw above with Hershovitz, this view is often partly motivated by a commitment to holding that "obligation" has the same meaning in sentences like (1) and (2)—though it is far from clear why the datum that "obligation" has the same meaning supports the inference that it has a *moral* meaning in (1). The idea that "obligation" could simply have a generic meaning seems to be ignored. It is worth stressing how odd that is. For instance, taking "obligation" to always have a moral meaning suggests that modifying "obligation" with "moral" is strictly redundant.[38]

What about the univocality of "legal?" Recall (9): "Positivism is a theory of legal institutions and obligations." It is awkward at best to say "legal" here marks the law's perspective about institutions. Andrew Currie (2020: 121–122) similarly notes that "I have a legal question" does not literally mean that "The law claims that I have a moral question." There is also a further problem posed by examples like (9). Proponents of the view in question, like Gardner (2012), explain the law's perspective *in terms of* legal officials and legal institutions. So, when "legal" modifies "institutions," does it mark the law's perspective *about* institutions? Circularity looms. It is, notably, hard to find analogous cases for words like "Kantian" which mark the perspective of a moral theory about something like *institutions* or *questions*. Proponents of this view, then, need to do one of two things: either they need an explanation for why "legal" marks the perspective of a moral theory only when it modifies some words like "obligation"; or they need to explain why it similarly marks the perspective of a moral theory when it modifies "question," "institution," and a whole range of non-normative vocabulary.

---

[38] Wodak (2018: 797) discusses this more. That moral perspectivalists hold the radical view that "ought" (etc.) always has a moral meaning is at least implicit when, e.g., Shapiro says: "When claims sans the word 'legal' are made, they express propositions with moral significance. To say that you are obligated to pay your taxes, for example, implies that you morally ought to pay your taxes. When the word 'legal' is used to preface the use of normative terminology, the speaker might be either expressing her judgment about a moral reason for action (namely, that the reason results from the operation of a legal institution) or exploiting the perspectival interpretation of the word" (2011: 191). See also Raz (1984: 131) and Gardner (2012: 37). Judith Jarvis Thomson (2008) also held that "ought" and "obligation" have a moral meaning. For a response pointing out the "absurd consequences" of this view, see Finlay (2014: 235–236).

To see why this is a serious challenge, it is worth comparing the issue to how the Kratzerian view (Section 2) explains why "legal" marks an ordering source when it modifies "obligation," but not when it modifies "institution." The answer is that terms like "obligation," unlike "institution," are always relative to a contextually salient ordering source. The modifier "legal" makes this contribution when modifying "obligation" because of a stable feature of the semantics of "obligation." By contrast, it is not a stable feature of the meaning of "obligation" that it is always relative to a *theoretical perspective*. This is why the challenge for moral perspectivalism is much harder to meet. What can they say to explain why "legal" modifies the meaning of "obligation" to mark a theoretical perspective, but does not generally mark a theoretical perspective?

Embedding

Moral perspectivalism also faces a serious challenge with embedding. This is, in fact, the source of a recent objection from Adam Perry: moral "perspectivalism is unable to account for the use of legal claims in logically complex arguments" (2023: 718).

Perry's argument concerns the example of (11)–(13): "All and only persons over 18 have a legal right to vote"; "A has a legal right to vote"; "So, A is over 18." The problem, Perry notes, is that this argument is invalid under perspectivalism. The literal meaning of (11) becomes "According to law all and only persons over 18 have a moral right to vote," and (12) becomes "According to law A has a moral right to vote." But if this is the literal meaning of sentences (11) and (12), they do not entail (13). As Perry notes, "the invalidity is obvious" when we consider structurally analogous cases where the relevant point of view is false, and the legal point of view is meant to be fallible.[39]

Perry considers a way around this problem by appealing to two commitments. The first is to say that the legal point of view is deductively closed. Perry considers the following closure rule: "If p is entailed by $q, r, s, \ldots$, and according to law each of $q, r, s, \ldots$, then according to law p" (2023: 720). But Perry notes that this closure rule "leads to absurd results" for moral perspectivalism. Suppose being a competent adult entails being morally obligated to keep your promises. If, according to the law, you are a competent adult, and what's true according to the law is closed under the rule just specified, then according to the law, you have a moral obligation to keep your promises. For moral perspectivalists, this means that you now have a legal obligation to keep your promises!

---

[39] Here's Perry's example: "According to my neighbour all and only those who are lizards disguised as humans are morally permitted to lie"; "According to my neighbour I am morally permitted to lie"; "So, I am a lizard disguised as a human." If the premises are true, they do not entail the (false) conclusion.

That is absurd. But it is not clear whether this problem stems from the specific closure rule that Perry considers. Arguably, the moral perspectivalists can endorse a weaker closure rule; the Kantian moral theory seems to be closed under entailment in some sense, but it is not clear that it is closed under the rule Perry considers above.[40]

The second commitment is that (13) is implicitly prefixed ("So, according to law A is over 18"). Perry seems to treat this commitment as innocuous, but it strikes me as *ad hoc*. Why say the *literal meaning* of (13) is prefixed when it is preceded by legal premises? Suppose we replace "legal" with "moral" in the premises (11) and (12). Unless we also adopt a perspectivalist semantics for moral language, we do not need to similarly say that the literal meaning of (13) is prefixed for the argument to be valid. Nor should we say that. It seems bizarre to hold that when it is accompanied by (11) and (12), (13) literally means "According to law, A is over 18," but if we replace "legal" with "moral" in (11) and (12), (13) literally means "According to morality, A is over 18." The literal meaning of "A is over 18" isn't prefixed, and it is *ad hoc* to say that the way it is prefixed as a conclusion depends on whether "legal" or "moral" appears in the premises.

Where does this leave moral perspectivalists? Notice that *both* moves must work to block Perry's objection. If moral perspectivalists can endorse a suitable closure rule that does not have absurd implications, that helps them explain why the argument is valid *only if* the conclusion of the argument is implicitly prefixed. So they face an uphill battle.

Linguistic Data

Moral perspectivalism says that "legal" modifies "obligation" in the same way that "Kantian" modifies "obligation" in sentences like (17). How can we test this?

Wodak (2018: 801–802) offered a way. Consider how we can stack the modifiers "Kantian" and "moral," as in: "You have a Kantian moral obligation not to lie." There is nothing unacceptable about this sentence; stacking "Kantian" and "moral" just clarifies that the Kantian point of view is a perspective about morality. This generates a testable prediction: if "legal" and "Kantian" modify "obligation" in the same way, we should similarly be able to stack "legal" and "moral." But when we do so, we generate semantically anomalous sentences like (14): "You have a legal moral obligation to pay taxes." This sentence can only be ascribed a bizarre meaning.

---

[40] Cf. Gardner (2012: ch. 1), Currie (2020: 145–164). See especially Ryu and Sewell (forthcoming).

It is worth noting two points about such linguistic data. First, perspectival modifiers can typically be stacked the same way as "Kantian" above. In the following normative and non-normative examples, the addition of the modifier in parentheses does not produce semantically anomalous sentences: "You have a utilitarian (moral) obligation to pay taxes"; and "You have a putative (moral) obligation to pay taxes"; "The duality of waves and particles is an Einsteinian (scientific) fact." By contrast, stacking modifiers of "obligation" that mark distinct ordering sources typically does produce semantically anomalous sentences: "You have a moral prudential obligation to pay taxes." This broader diet of examples adds considerable weight to the relevant linguistic data.

Second, moral perspectivalists are under significant pressure to explain such data. Moral perspectivalists could brush off such data if they were engaged in, say, analyzing the illocutionary force of sentences like (2), or offering an account of the pragmatics rather than semantics of sentences like (2).[41] But its key proponents, like Raz and Shapiro, advance this theory to support a solution to the challenge posed by Hume's is/ought gap (see Section 6). As such, moral perspectivalism must be understood as offering exactly what it says on the tin: an account of the semantics of sentences like (1).[42] But a central desideratum for a semantic theory is that it accords with linguistic data.

These two points show that moral perspectivalists need to explain linguistic data about modifier stacking, but have no clear path to do so.[43] But these points also suggest something methodologically awry about moral perspectivalism. This is first and foremost a semantic theory. So, any proponent of the theory should have been considering what distinctive testable predictions it makes about linguistic data. Proponents of the theory have offered no response to a challenge about such predictions. Worse yet, they never sought to elicit any testable predictions in the first place. This observation is about as damning as the data from sentences like (14).

It is worth emphasizing that the problems with embedding and linguistic data target different components of moralized perspectivalism. The view faces

---

[41] Asgeirsson (2020: ch. 1) takes the lesson of Wodak (2018) to be that moralized perspectivalism fares better as an account of the pragmatics rather than semantics of sentences like (1). Cf. Wodak (2021: 778).

[42] I'll briefly spell this out without delving into the putative problem posed by Hume's is/ought gap (§VI). Suppose you thought that it would be a problem if legal obligations exist and facts about legal obligations were fully grounded in descriptive social facts. Raz and Shapiro try to solve that problem is by offering an account of the semantics of all sentences like (1) such that they do not existentially commit to distinctively legal obligations, and correspond to descriptive facts about what obligations exist according to a theory. They could not solve that problem by offering an account of anything like the illocutionary force of (1).

[43] I thank Brian Leiter, Alma Diamond, and their class at the University of Chicago for a very helpful discussion about the last two points.

a problem with embedding because it is *perspectival* (it takes "legal" to semantically mark a point of view); and it faces a problem with modifier stacking because it is *moral* (it takes this "obligation" to mean "moral obligation"). Each commitment, then, is dubious.

Psychological Plausibility

What about internal and external statements? Internal legal statements, recall, are normative statements made from the point of view of an adherent of a legal system. If we suppose that the legal point of view is a moral theory, then internal legal statements seem to express adherence to that moral theory. That is also how proponents of moral perspectivalism understand the internal point of view. Raz, for example, suggests that "judges believe that legal obligations are morally binding," and this is "what they actually say when asserting obligations according to the law" (1984: 131).[44] Internal legal statements express the internal point of view; so the internal point of view is moral.

Taking the internal point of view to be moral is independently controversial.[45] But there is also a reason to think it is incompatible with moral perspectivalists' commitments. This reason again concerns legal permissions, in simple sentences such as (5): "People are legally permitted to commit adultery." I assume (5) is true. I also assume judges think it is true. A judge may say (5) from the bench if, for example, someone is accused of adultery and the judge wants to point out that they are not thereby accused of a crime. But according to moral perspectivalism, (5) literally means that according to the legal point of view, people are morally permitted to commit adultery. By parity of reasoning, such a judge *expresses the belief that adultery is morally permissible*, and this is what they actually say when asserting its permissibility according to the law.[46]

This implication is hard to swallow. And the bullet is harder to bite when we reflect on two points. First, adultery is just one example. On this view, someone who accepts the law as a system of norms thereby accepts that *everything* the law does not forbid is morally permissible. And as Matthew Etchemendy notes

---

[44] This generalization at least appears to admit of many exceptions. See e.g., Cover (1975).
[45] Toh develops several lines of objections against this commitment. See Toh (2005, 2007, 2011).
[46] Granted, moral perspectivalists could say that (5) means there is a weak legal permission to commit adultery. Currie notes that this view provides the resources to distinguish "between strong and weak legal-deontic modalities" (2020: 136 ff). The problem raised in the main text above is acute in cases where the best interpretation is that a judge is asserting strong legal permission—i.e., where the law's theory says that an act is not obligatory, rather than where it is merely not the case that the law's theory says that an act is obligatory. (Such cases should not be hard to come by.) Currie also offers a rich discussion (2020: 144–145) of why moral perspectivalists face challenges with respect to weak and strong deontic modalities.

in a related context, "committing adultery" is "perfectly legal in a wide range of circumstances," along with plenty of other "nasty or pointlessly destructive things" such as "gratuitously insulting loyal friends" (2018: 19). If we accept moral perspectivalism, the internal point of view looks pathological. Second, a theory that holds that everything not legally prohibited is morally permitted has implausible substantive commitments *and structural* features. It will not treat morally like cases alike, since the law's prohibitions are selective.

How, then, should we regard the dominant semantic theory from positivists? Taken on its own, the theory fails to satisfy basic desiderata. But we should also evaluate the theory comparatively. That is, how does the theory fare in comparison to its rivals? The Kratzerian view, by contrast, seems to avoid its pitfalls because it takes "obligation" to have a generic rather than moral meaning, and because it takes "legal" and "moral" to modify "obligation" the same way: "legal" marks a distinct ordering source, like "moral," rather than a theoretical perspective on morality.

4 Hooray for Law

The next most prominent positivist position is an *expressivist* semantics for "legal obligation." Kevin Toh offers the most developed expressivist view (2005, 2011, 2013). Here is how one critic, Matthew Kramer, glossed this position:

> [E]very such [internal legal] statement is relevantly similar to other utterances whose semantic contents are filled entirely by their non-cognitive pragmatics. In other words, every internal legal statement is relevantly similar to utterances such as "Hurray for the Boston Celtics" or [...] "Wow" or "Oh boy" or "Hello" or "Shut the door." No such utterance is appropriately evaluable as true or false, and the meaning of each such utterance is given entirely by its expression of an emotion or a desire or some other non-cognitive attitude (2018: 404).

The existing literature is somewhat preoccupied with whether an expressivist view should be attributed to Hart. Toh, along with Raz (1981: 448–449), Shapiro (2006: 1169–1170, 2011: 98–99), and others,[47] interpret Hart as an expressivist; Kramer, along with Finlay and Plunkett (2018), resists this interpretation. (More accurately: everyone agrees that Hart was initially an expressivist, but they disagree on whether Hart renounced or retained this view in later work.)[48] I want to set this aside and focus instead on the more important issue:

---

[47] See Toh (2013: 467), Etchemendy (2016: 1–2 and fn. 1), and the references in both.
[48] See, e.g., Kramer (2018: 406): "Hart in a few of his very early writings did propound some non-cognitivist analyses of the contents of certain internal legal statements," citing (Hart 1949, 1983, chap. 1).

Is expressivism true? Or, more modestly: How favorably does expressivism about "legal obligation" compare to rival semantics theories?

Let's start by outlining the view. Kramer's gloss above is rough and arguably uncharitable. I will initially outline the core commitments of the view while bracketing some significant qualifications and questions, then provide a more careful exposition of what expressivists are committed to about sentences like (1): "You have a legal obligation to pay taxes." I'll also stress that I focus here on the commitments of Allan Gibbard's expressivist project, which provide the foundations for legal expressivism.[49]

The two central commitments of the expressivist view are that we explain the meaning of sentences like (1) via identifying the attitudes that they express, and that (the relevant uses of) sentences like (1) express the speaker's acceptance of the relevant legal norms. Since these states of acceptance are non-cognitive, they are not capable of being true or false; so (the relevant uses of) sentences like (1) turn out to be neither true nor false.

This initial outline is enough to see that expressivism is a radical departure from a truth-conditional semantics for sentences like (1).[50] The point of departure is not in holding that there are some sentences that are not truth-apt. It is uncontroversial to hold that some sentences—e.g., "Wow" or "Shut the door"—are not truth-apt. What is controversial is holding that "You have a legal obligation to pay taxes," unlike other sentences with a similar syntactic form, is semantically like "Wow" or "Shut the door" in this respect. To that extent, Kramer's characterization of the view is fair. But Kramer overstates the extent to which expressivists treat (1) as akin to "Wow." Contemporary expressivists tend to hold that (the relevant uses of) sentences like (1) express a complex practical attitude. Toh calls the attitude in question "plural norm acceptance," and characterizes it as follows: "Let us φ, on the assumption that: you, of your own accord, think or will come to think likewise!"[51] Leaving aside the details of Toh's proposal, the point is that if expressivists explain the meaning of (the relevant uses of) sentences like (1) in terms of the non-cognitive attitudes

---

[49] See e.g., Toh (2005: 78). I leave open whether the problems for Gibbardian expressivism are solvable on different ways of developing expressivist accounts, especially Yalcin's account (2012), which Toh appealed to in a response to a draft of this chapter (p.c.). See Dowell (2024) for a careful, optimistic take on how Yalcin's view can handle problems with compositionality. I set this Yalcin's view aside not only for brevity, but because it is not strictly an expressivist *semantics*. (As Dowell writes: "Yalcin's expressivism is captured by his pragmatics"; "There is nothing particularly expressivist about Yalcin's semantics.") If legal expressivism takes Yalcin's expressivism as its starting point, it is arguably a pragmatic rather than semantic theory.

[50] See Schroeder (2008) on expressivism as a radical departure from truth-conditional semantics.

[51] Toh (2011: 120; see also 122).

that they express *while taking these attitudes to be complex*, they say (1) is more semantically complex than "Wow."

Now let's turn to the qualifications and questions. First, as is parenthetically indicated above, expressivists do not defend a non-cognitivist account of *all* legal statements. So, what are the relevant uses of statements like (1)? Toh's expressivism provides a non-cognitivist account of the semantics for *committed internal legal statements*. A statement like (1) counts among this class when it is made by an adherent of the legal system.

Here's how Toh (2011: 109) introduces the expressivist view about such statements:

> [E]xpressions containing deontic terms such as "ought", "may", "obligatory", etc. are often ambiguous. A speaker, in saying "Smoking is prohibited", for instance, may be making a *normative* or *prescriptive* statement, thus putting demands on others to stop (or not start) smoking. Or he may be making a *descriptive* statement, thus characterizing a state of affairs in which a relevant group of people adhere to a norm against smoking.

Toh continues that "typical legal expressions," like "The Fourteenth Amendment allows states to regulate bakery employees' work hours," are similarly "ambiguous": They "can be interpreted as normative statements or as descriptive statements." And Toh also notes an "analogous distinction" in moral sentences like "Lying is wrong." This string of words can be a committed internal moral statement or an external moral statement.

What, then, does the expressivist say about the meaning of other uses of sentences like (1)? Toh writes: "The meaning of committed internal legal statements, I am assuming, is primary in the sense that the meanings of external legal statements [...] can be understood as parasitic on the meaning of the former" (2011: 110). For Toh, "external legal statements are in large part *attributions* of norm-acceptances and of their expression" (2011: n. 5).[52] Toh has not said much more about external legal statements. But as Matthew Etchemendy notes, "the basic idea seems to be that an external legal statement is a descriptive generalization about the 'internal' legal judgments of the members of some relevant reference population" (2016: 10). This basic idea is analogous, Etchemendy writes, to what some metaethical non-cognitivists describe as "inverted commas" uses of ethical terms: for example, an anthropologist who says "infanticide was morally permissible in Sparta" may express "the belief that Spartans generally thought that infanticide was morally

---

[52] For brevity and clarity, I am omitting what Toh says about detached legal statements (2007, 2013).

Law's Language 31

permissible." Similarly, then, external legal statements describe others' psychological attitudes toward the law.[53]

So, those are the relevant uses of (1). Let's turn to the second qualification: What is it that the expressivist takes these uses of (1) to express, and hence to *mean*? I noted that Toh takes internal legal statements to express plural norm acceptance. (As an aside: Some use "acceptance" to refer to a cognitive attitude, but throughout this section, I use "acceptance" to refer to the specific type of non-cognitive attitude that Toh has in mind.) But this leaves the question: What exactly is accepted? Etchemendy describes Toh's "brief remarks" on this issue as "puzzling and quite unsatisfactory."[54]

There's a straightforward option for expressivists here. Since (1) is "You have a legal obligation to pay taxes," the expressivist can say it expresses acceptance of *your paying taxes*: i.e., "A legally must φ" expresses plural norm acceptance of A φing. A variant of this option takes into account that (1) is a particular instance of a general obligation (e.g., citizens and residents have a legal obligation to pay taxes). The expressivist can say that the relevant uses of (1) express acceptance of the general, rather than particular, content of that legal obligation (e.g., acceptance of *citizens and residents* paying taxes).

There are also less straightforward alternatives. Those who flout the law are liable to punishment by the state. So the expressivist could say the relevant uses of (1) express the acceptance of *your being punished if you do not pay taxes*. Or, more generally, it may express acceptance of citizens and residents being punished if they do not pay taxes. Similar views are suggested by Hart (1982) and Etchemendy (2016: 20).

There are other options. But the general point is that if we are to use expressivism to understand the literal meaning of "A legally must φ," we need to know more than what *type* of attitude it expresses; we also need to know the *content* of that attitude. Since the expressivist posits that "A legally must φ" expresses a practical attitude, or an attitude *which guides action*, we need to know what action(s) feature in its content.

But suppose we restrict ourselves to these options. How should the expressivist decide between them? "Judging that the law requires citizens to pay taxes to the government may motivate someone to pay her taxes," Finlay and Plunkett

---

[53] Toh (p.c.) similarly says that we can understand external legal statements as being akin to the use of "free indirect style" in literary theory: where a speaker speaks "from attributees' standpoint" but drops "the quotation marks and attitude verbs." So external legal statements are elliptical attitude reports.

[54] Etchemendy continues "Even if a legal statement expresses not just the acceptance of a particular norm N but also the acceptance of certain norms about how N is to be 'modified' or how disputes about N's applicability are to be resolved, we should like to know what the content of N itself is" (2016: 18).

note, and expressivism, they say, is "tailor-made for explaining the practical uses of legal statements" (2018: 49–50). As is often true in tailoring, the details matter. If expressivists say committed internal legal statements like "The law requires citizens to pay taxes" express the conditional acceptance of *punishment*, how does it explain why such a judgment motivates one *to pay taxes*? It suggests one is motivated by the fear of punishment, which risks defining out of existence the internal point of view—citizens who follow the law solely to avoid sanctions constitute a paradigm case of the *external* point of view.

A further advantage of the straightforward view is that it skirts some tricky problems. Consider the majority judgment in *Vieth v. Jubelier*, 124 S. Ct. 1769 (2004): Partisan gerrymandering is unconstitutional, but it is nonjusticiable, as the Supreme Court lacks a judicially manageable standard. Presuming that the Supreme Court Justices take the internal point of view, what practical attitude do they express in their judgment? The answer does not seem to be the acceptance of a *sanction* conditional on gerrymandering.

There's more to be said here, and generally, the core features of the expressivist view need to be more clearly hashed out. Defenders of the view do not seem to disagree with that assessment. Toh is refreshingly modest in noting that "[f]ar more will need to be said to defend [the view] adequately" (2011: 134), and Etchemendy, who is sympathetic to the view, writes that "legal expressivism is in its infancy" (2016: 3). We'll see some further choice points for anyone interested in developing this theory as we turn to evaluating how expressivism fares in relation to the five desiderata from Section 1.

Scope

If expressivism is a theory of the meaning of "legal obligation," then, as Etchemendy notes, the expressivist also needs a theory of the meaning of "statements like 'you have a legal right to dispose of your own property,' and any number of other kinds of internal legal statements" (2016: 19 fn. 56). Toh seems to agree; after all, Toh explicitly takes the expressivist view to have a scope that includes statements like "The Fourteenth Amendment allows states to regulate bakery employees' work hours." This example involves language of permission, just like (5): "People are legally permitted to commit adultery." So the expressivist needs an account of the practical attitude that is expressed by committed internal statements of (5), and how it relates to the practical attitude that is expressed by committed internal statements of (1).

I will again focus on statements about legal permissions rather than (say) legal rights, because it draws out a general problem for the theory. If "Legally,

A must φ" expresses plural norm acceptance of A φing, what exactly do sentences like "Legally, A can φ" and "Legally, A cannot φ" express? Expressivists struggle to provide plausible answers that explain which of these sentences are consistent and inconsistent.

The main difficulty is familiar from discussions of how metaethical expressivists should handle negation. Here's how Mark Schroeder explains that general problem:

> There are three places to insert a negation in 'Jon thinks that murdering is wrong', all of which receive distinct semantic interpretations:
> w   Jon thinks that murdering is wrong.
> n1   Jon does not think that murdering is wrong.
> n2   Jon thinks that murdering is not wrong.
> n3   Jon thinks that not murdering is wrong.
> Sentence n1 denies Jon a positive view about the wrongness of murdering, n2 attributes to Jon a negative view about the wrongness of murdering, and n3 attributes to Jon a positive view about the wrongness of not murdering. According to n2, he thinks that murdering is permissible, whereas according to n3 he thinks that it is obligatory. Conflating any two of these three would be a disaster.
>
> Yet that is precisely the danger for expressivists. For according to expressivism, thinking that murdering is wrong is being in the mental state expressed by 'murdering is wrong'. That is, it is disapproving of murdering. But there are simply not enough places to insert a negation in 'Jon disapproves of murdering':
> w*   Jon disapproves of murdering.
> n1* Jon does not disapprove of murdering.
> n2* ???
> n3* Jon disapproves of not murdering.
> There is simply one place not enough for the negations to go around. There is no way to account for the meaning of n2 by applying 'not' somewhere to the meaning of w. And that makes it look very much like expressivists are not going to be able to offer a satisfactory explanation of why 'murder is wrong' and 'murder is not wrong' are inconsistent (2008: 44–45).

Legal expressivists need to explain the semantic relation between "legal obligation" and "legal permission": if it is true that "You are legally obligated to pay taxes," then it is false that "You are legally permitted to not pay taxes" (Section 1). And if they are to explain this in terms of the attitudes that committed internal uses of these sentences express, then the attitude expressed by the first sentence needs to be inconsistent with the attitude expressed by the second. As Schroder writes:

> Some actions are permissible without being obligatory—i.e., it is permissible both to do them and to not do them. So 'not murdering is not wrong'

('not murdering is permissible') is consistent with 'murdering is not wrong', but inconsistent with 'not murdering is wrong' ('murdering is obligatory'). So 'not murdering is not wrong' must express a state of mind that is *consistent* with the state of mind expressed by 'murdering is not wrong', but *inconsistent* with the state of mind expressed by 'not murdering is wrong' (2008: 46).

Suppose, then, that Toh holds that "You are legally obligated to pay taxes" expresses the attitude of acceptance of your paying taxes. This must be *consistent* with the attitude that is expressed by "You are legally permitted to pay taxes," as well as *inconsistent* with the attitude that is expressed by "You are legally permitted not to pay taxes." As Schroeder's discussion above outlines, legal expressivists here face the problem that when we run through the available options, there are not enough spots for the "not."

There is also a way that the problem posed here for expressivists about legal language is harder than the problem for expressivists about moral language. The legal expressivist needs to explain the *inconsistency* of the attitudes expressed in "You are legally permitted to φ" and "You are not legally permitted to φ," while explaining the *consistency* of the attitudes expressed by "Law X permits φing" and "Law Y does not permit φing." If these are committed internal statements that express practical attitudes—attitudes like desires, whose contents are actions—it is not immediately clear how the expressivist can generate the result that the first pair of sentences expresses inconsistent attitudes but the similar pair of sentences expresses consistent attitudes.

I do not mean for this to convey that these problems are insoluble. Indeed, there are interesting recent proposals in metaethics that take expressivism in a different direction in an attempt to solve this problem—see, e.g., Incurvati and Schlöder (2021). These proposals might provide new resources for legal expressivists. But however, the view is developed, it needs to explain the broad scope of prescriptive legal language.

Univocality

Expressivism faces a further challenge with the univocality of "obligation." In fact, it faces a harder challenge on this front than any theory we considered so far.

In discussing this issue in Section 1, I noted that the same term, "obligation," appears in legal language, in moral language, and in mixed language. The examples of this were (1), (2), and (6): "You have a legal obligation to pay taxes," "You have a moral obligation to pay taxes," and "You have a moral and legal obligation to pay taxes." As we saw, sentences like (6) provide evidence that "obligation" is univocal in (1) and (2). That is, "obligation" has the same meaning when it is modified by "legal" and "moral."

Expressivism is inconsistent with this. It is even inconsistent with something more basic: that "legal obligation" is univocal in (1), and that "moral obligation" is univocal in (2). We saw above that Toh makes this explicit: "expressions containing deontic terms such as 'ought', 'may', 'obligatory', etc. are often ambiguous." Here Toh cites with approval Eugenio Bulygin's 'Norms, Normative Propositions, and Legal Statements', which endorses the view that "deontic sentences"—that is, "sentences in which such deontic terms as 'ought', 'may', 'obligatory', 'forbidden', 'permitted', and so on occur"—"are typically ambiguous" (2015 [1982]: 188). Toh does not just happen to endorse this stance. It falls out of the expressivist semantic program, as Toh understands it. The expressivist offers a non-cognitivist semantics for *committed internal statements*; external statements are said to differ in meaning. So, for the expressivist, terms like "ought," "must," "can," "obligation," and "permission" are not univocal in legal language like (1), or in moral language like (2), let alone in mixed uses like (6). Whether or not Hart is an expressivist, Hart also seemed to flatly deny "the identity of meaning of 'obligation' in moral and legal contexts,"[55] and many take that to be Hart's considered view.[56] This would suggest that Hart similarly denies the univocality of "obligation" in (6) and hence predicts that its use in that sentence is zeugmatic.[57]

The expressivist's commitment to ambiguity is a radical departure from a Kratzerian view (Section 2). As I noted, on Kratzer's semantics, deontic modals are univocal. Indeed, on this view, *modals* are univocal. That is: "must" has the same meaning not only when it is used in relation to duty, but when it is used in relation to *necessity*, be it deontic, logical, metaphysical, epistemic, or what have you. When we compare the expressivist view to its Kratzerian rival with respect to univocality, they could not be further apart.

For three reasons, I think this constitutes a significant vice of an expressivist semantic program, and a substantial relative virtue of a univocal semantics, like Kratzer's. First, as we saw, it is standardly thought that the onus is on those who

---

[55] Hart (1982: 159–160). This evidence is somewhat murky; Hart is arguably saying that *if* one accepts certain Razian commitments about the meaning of "moral obligation," then it is better to deny this claim about the identity of meaning than to endorse a similar view about the meaning of "moral obligation."

[56] Timothy Endicott: "According to Hart, the meaning of normative language differs in morality and in law. But in fact, Hart had nothing to say about the *meaning* of normative expressions such as 'ought' and 'must' or 'obligation' or 'right' (except that their meaning differs in law and in morality)" (2022: §6.2, emphasis in original). Kramer also says that "Hart disagreed with Raz over the notion that a single concept of obligation is shared between legal discourse and moral discourse" (2018: 408).

[57] Hart (1982: 127) says that Kelsen and Holmes took this view. And Richard Holton similarly holds that "obligatory" has different meanings in "legally obligatory" and "morally obligatory" (1998: 617). But Holton's stance here seems to hinge on confusing *truth-conditions* with *grounds* (Wodak 2018: 805).

posit lexical ambiguities to proffer linguistic data that supports their position. Toh does not offer any evidence from any standard test for lexical ambiguity. Nor do other expressivists. As we saw in Section 1, such tests support univocality, not such profligate ambiguity.

Insofar as evidence is offered for the claim that deontic terms are "typically ambiguous," it seems to be of the wrong kind. In a telling moment, Bulygin moves from a claim about "the ambiguity of deontic expressions" to a claim about "the practical difficulty of determining *which speech act or acts* have been performed on a given occasion" (2015 [1982]: 198–199, emphasis mine).[58] This seems to confuse the orthodoxy that a single utterance of (1) can constitute multiple speech acts with the heterodoxy that there is no univocal semantics for a single sentence like (1). Toh (2005: 96–99) similarly holds that the development of J.L. Austin's speech act theory was a major influence on Hart's views about the semantics of legal obligation, and Toh appeals to Austin's speech act theory extensively. But as I noted in Section 1, Austin's speech act theory is based on the distinction between locutionary, illocutionary, and perlocutionary acts—where only locutionary acts relate to literal meaning. The claim that an utterance of (1) can constitute different kinds of speech acts is *not* equivalent to the claim that the single sentence (1) has multiple literal meanings depending on the speaker's attitudes.

Second, a view that holds that deontic terms are univocal will be more parsimonious than a view that holds that they are ambiguous. Again, we are finite creatures. Our brains are limited. As Kratzer notes, we use "must" and "obligation" to refer to many different kinds of duties. If obligation is not univocal in (1), in (2), or in (6), then as we consider more examples of normative language, we soon get the result that our brains must somehow learn, store, and aptly deploy many multitudes of meanings for each deontic term. Toh could say something to soften the force of this blow. Toh writes:

> my ambition is not to explain all of legal discourse. Instead, it is to provide an analysis of what I there called "committed internal legal statements". The conjecture I am working with is that a satisfactory analysis of such statements

---

[58] This confusion does, I think, lie at the heart of Bulygin's article. Right after the passage just quoted, Bulygin discusses the "ambiguity of the term 'valid', and hence of statements of the form 'this rule (statute,contract) is valid.'" Sometimes, in "saying 'this statute is valid', one is simply recording the fact that it has been duly enacted by the legislature, but this would be an external statement of fact"; at other times, "[t]o say 'this contact is valid' [...] is tantamount to saying that you must do what this contract stipulates; the statement is to prescribe a certain form of conduct, but it does not describe anything at all" (2015 [1982]: 199). What people are "saying" in an utterance is not equivalent to its literal meaning.

would be explanatorily primary in the sense that analyses of other kinds of legal statements would depend on it whereas it would not depend on those other analyses. (2011: 125).

If the meaning of external uses of "legal obligation" is derivative of the meaning of committed internal uses of the same phrase, the proliferation of lexical entries may be less dire: we still have distinct meanings for "legal obligation," but at least they are related. (In other words, "legal obligation" would be *polysemous*.) Similarly, we would get distinct but related meanings for "moral obligation," and for "grammatical requirement," and so on. But the real problem, I think, is that "obligation" still has a distinct meaning in (6), and ditto for "requirement" in a mixed use like "moral and grammatical requirement," and so on. At best, this move makes a vice somewhat less vicious; but it does not come close to turning that vice into a virtue.

Third, if "obligation" is not univocal in (1), it becomes harder to explain disagreement. Toh takes it to be an ambition of the expressivist program to "make sense of legal disagreements between people who subscribe to different fundamental norms" (2011: 116). So suppose Mitch says (1) and Kim responds by asserting ~(1)—that is, "You do not have a legal obligation to pay taxes." They disagree. This remains the case even if Mitch takes the external point of view and Kim takes the internal point of view, or vice versa. As Finlay and Plunkett note, "expressivists like Toh seem committed to a separate account of the semantics of external statements of law, and therefore are hard-pressed to explain how such disagreements are possible" (2018: 70). Why is that? We saw that Toh takes the external legal statements, as Etchemendy wrote, to be akin to anthropologist claiming "Infanticide was morally permissible in Sparta." If an anthropologist said that and someone responded, "No, infanticide was morally impermissible in Sparta!", they would be talking past each other. The confusion could be cleared up by the anthropologist: "I simply meant that Spartans generally thought that infanticide was morally permissible." The disagreement between Mitch and Kim does not seem similar to this exchange. They do not seem to be talking past each other, and neither could say anything similar to the anthropologists' clarification to clarify their merely verbal dispute, because their dispute is not merely verbal.[59]

---

[59] Toh seems to agree, to a point. Enoch and Toh write that legal "insiders and outsiders can, and often actually do, engage each other in meaningful discussions about what the law is, or about which norms are legally valid. And they do not seem to be talking past each other when they do" (2013: 258). But they go on to note that Enoch "is inclined to view Hart's distinction [between internal and external legal judgments] as ill-drawn, for it seems to find an ambiguity where none exists," whereas Toh "is somewhat more sanguine about Hart's distinction between internal and external legal judgments, and the corresponding distinction between internal and external legal statements. It seems quite true that people who are committed to the laws of their legal system and those who are disaffected or uncommitted may hold a conversation about whether a certain

Perhaps, then, the expressivist should change course. What if expressivists instead aim to offer a univocal semantics for "obligation" in (1), (2), and (6)? This is no easy task. In fact, they face at least two hurdles in trying to pull it off.

First, let's consider how the expressivists can explain the univocality of "obligation" in (1). Suppose, that is, one endorsed an expressivist view about internal and external statements of (1). Some have suggested (sloppily, I think) that Hart held this view.[60]

The main obstacle to this view is that expressivists aim to explain the meaning of sentences in terms of the attitudes that they express, and hold that *internal* statements of (1) express a practical attitude, norm-acceptance, but those who take the *external* point of view lack that attitude. Expressivists would now need to say that any utterance of (1) expresses the attitude of norm-acceptance even when the speaker does not have that attitude. To take this stance is to say that external legal statements are like fake smiles: They express an attitude that the speaker lacks, so they are *insincere*. But to simply assert this is to posit insincerity without evidence. That's little better than positing lexical ambiguity without evidence. We need an argument for why (1) has these sincerity conditions, and one that tracks the typical ways of determining sincerity conditions in philosophy of language. The violation of sincerity conditions typically makes a speech act *infelicitous*. If you promise to read my draft but have no intention of doing so, your promise is insincere and so infelicitous. It is, in the parlance of speech act theory, an *abuse*. But if someone who takes the external point of view says, "You have a legal obligation to pay taxes," their speech act does not seem infelicitous.[61] So if the expressivist says

---

act is legal, without thereby equivocating and talking past each other. But what this data may motivate is not so much the conclusion that (what Hart calls) internal and external legal statements have the same meaning, but instead that people (or more specifically, participants) may utter internal legal statements and thereby display their endorsements or commitments either sincerely or insincerely" (2013: 268–69).

[60] Shapiro (2006: 1169, internal references omitted) writes: "Hart's semantic program might be described as being a mixture of cognitivism and non-cognitivism. With respect to understanding assertions about the existence of secondary legal rules, such as the rule of recognition, Hart is a cognitivist. These statements state propositions and, hence, are capable of being true or false. This cognitivism rests on a reductive account of social rules. For Hart, a social rule just is a social practice and, hence, to say that the rule of recognition exists is simply to state that a certain regularity of behavior is generally accepted as a standard of conduct. With respect to statements about the existence of primary legal rules, on the other hand, Hart is a non-cognitivist. These statements do not state propositions and, hence, cannot be true or false. This particular brand of non-cognitivism is a form of norm-expressivism. To state that a legal rule is valid is to express the acceptance of a norm that requires that certain actions be followed." Since (1) is a statement of a primary rule, it follows that external statements of (1) also express norm-acceptance. See also Kramer (2018: 411–413) on the limited role of the rule of recognition in internal legal statements.

[61] The problem is actually worse than this. As I noted above, the expressivist needs to identify the *type and content* of the practical attitude that is expressed by "Legally, A must φ." Any utterance

internal and external legal statements are univocal in expressing the practical attitude of norm acceptance, then the expressivist faces an uphill battle in making a case for the surprising verdict that external legal statements are insincere.

The expressivist also faces a second hurdle when they turn to explaining the univocality of "obligation" in mixed sentences like (6). How can the expressivist capture the datum that "obligation" is univocal when it is modified by "moral" and "legal?" Wodak (2017) argued that expressivists here face a challenge in explaining univocality without over-generating semantic inconsistency.

There are two starting points for this argument. First, expressivists explain *sameness of meaning* in terms of *sameness of expressed attitudes*. If "obligation" has a univocal meaning in (6), then it must express acceptance when it is modified by "moral" and "legal." If "obligation" expresses acceptance when modified by "legal" and, say, hope when it is modified by "moral," the single use of "obligation" in (6) should seem zeugmatic. Second, expressivists explain the inconsistency of sentences in terms of the inconsistency of the attitudes those sentences express. Suppose the expressivist adopts what I described as the straightforward option above: "You have a legal obligation to pay taxes" expresses acceptance of your paying taxes. That sentence is inconsistent with "You do not have a legal obligation to pay taxes," so the negated sentence must express an attitude that is inconsistent with acceptance of your paying taxes. With these two starting points in mind, we can now consider a moral sentence like "You do not have a moral obligation to pay taxes." Why isn't the attitude that this sentence expresses also inconsistent with the attitude expressed by "You have a legal obligation to pay taxes?"

You might think that this problem is easy to resolve. The expressivist just needs to say that (1) and (2) express the same type of attitude, but with different contents. For example, Etchemendy finds it plausible that "A has moral obligation not to steal" expresses acceptance of blaming A if A steals,[62] while "A has a legal obligation not to steal" expresses acceptance of punishing A if A steals (2016: 16, 20). Many hold, however, that punishment constitutively involves

---

of that sentence by a speaker who lacks that highly specific attitude will be insincere, and hence infelicitous. This is true even if the speaker has a whole bunch of other positive attitudes toward the law and the legal system.

[62] This is roughly Gibbard's view in *Wise Choices, Apt Feelings*. "A morally ought to φ" expresses conditional plans to blame A if A φs. "A rationally ought to φ" expresses a plan for A to φ. Notice that on this view, "A morally ought to φ" is inconsistent with "I rationally ought not blame A if A φs."

the expression of blame. If that is true, then "A has legal obligation not to steal" expresses acceptance of punishing *and hence blaming* A if A steals. So it expresses an attitude that is inconsistent with the acceptance of not blaming A if A steals. More generally, it is hard to see how expressivists can offer a systematic explanation of why moral and legal claims are not inconsistent. Nothing on this view seems to guarantee that sentences like (7)—"People are legally, but not morally, permitted to commit adultery"—are never self-contradictory.

Interestingly, Toh grants that legal, moral, and even aesthetic judgments can all express the same specific type of practical attitude, plural norm acceptance (2011: 130). Toh then says this is not a problem because it "does not mean that all expressions of plural norm-acceptances, including legal statements, are a species of moral statements," and writes that there are likely to be "differences among the kinds of norms which are accepted in different kinds of normative judgments." That is, "A legally ought to φ," "A morally ought to φ," and "A aesthetically ought to φ" may all express plural norm acceptance, but will not all express plural norm acceptance *of A φing*. This doesn't help solve our problem. Suppose "A legally ought to φ" expresses acceptance of A φing and "A morally ought to φ" expresses acceptance of A ψing. These are consistent attitudes. But now ask: Why are "A legally ought to ψ" and "A morally ought to φ" consistent? Applying the view systematically, we still generate some unwanted inconsistencies.

Finally, there is a related question of whether the expressivist can explain the univocality of "legal" in sentences like (9): "Positivism is a theory of legal institutions and obligations." It is not clear what to make of these sentences. What does "legal" contribute when a single use of the word simultaneously modifies a term that expresses a non-cognitive attitude ("obligations") *and* a term that seems straightforwardly descriptive ("institutions")? Perhaps the expressivist will respond by also offering a non-cognitivist analysis of "institutions." But that response will struggle to be systematic. To modify Currie's earlier example: "I have so many legal questions and legal obligations" can be conjoined and reduced to "I have so many legal questions and obligations." Will we need to be expressivists about "questions" as well to make expressivism viable? Enoch and Toh "argue that *legal* is illuminatingly conceived as a thick concept," such that "declaring an act legal (or illegal) would involve an expression of some evaluative or normative commitment" (2013: 264–65). If *legal* is a thick concept, and we token that concept once in sentences (9), then it seems to follow, oddly, that declaring an institution or question to be legal similarly involves some normative commitment.

Embedding

The last two problems are serious. But we're only now coming to the most famous problem for expressivists, which concerns arguments like (11)–(13): "All and only persons over 18 have a legal right to vote"; "A has a legal right to vote," "So, A is over 18." The problem that examples like this generate is known as *the Frege-Geach problem*.[63] (The negation problem is really a special instance of the broader Frege-Geach problem.)

There are two aspects to Frege-Geach problem. First, if we suppose "A has a legal right to vote" expresses acceptance, and this captures its meaning, what does the sentence express and mean when it is embedded in a conditional? Consider, e.g., "If A has a legal right to vote, that's not good for your candidate's odds in November." It is hard to see how the expressivist account of the meaning of the bare asserted sentence is meant to relate to the meaning of the sentence when it is embedded (or conjoined, disjoined, etc.).

Second, how does the expressivist explain the validity of the inference to "A is over 18?" If "A has a legal right to vote" has a different meaning in the two premises, then the argument commits a fallacy of equivocation. More generally, if we understand validity in terms of truth-preservation—if the premises are true, the conclusion must be true—then how can the argument be valid if its premises are not truth-apt?

Toh writes that "Hart was aware of this second task involved in solving the Frege-Geach problem, and that he thought that it can be carried out to satisfaction," though Toh notes that Hart does not offer "a fully worked out proposal for a solution to the Frege-Geach problem" (2005: 104–05), and said little about the first task. As Kramer also notes (2018: 415), the kind of proposed solution that Hart built upon for the second task is at odds with Hart's own commitments about legal obligations (that they can conflict).

Of course, legal expressivists could seek solutions to this problem that have been developed elsewhere. But despite the enormous volume of work on the Frege-Geach problem over the past decades, not only is there no agreement about whether it has been solved, but "it remains highly controversial *whether it can be solved*" (Finlay and Plunkett 2018: 70, emphasis mine). It's not clear that we should be very optimistic about the prospects that legal expressivists will find or develop a solution.

---

[63] The contemporary discussion of the problem starts with Geach (1958).

Linguistic Data

Some argue that expressivism also faces problems with linguistic data. Jack Woods (2014) notes that expressivism predicts that some sentences should seem Moore-paradoxical, like "It's raining, but I don't believe that it's raining." If asserting *p* expresses the belief that *p*, the asserting *p but I don't believe that p* is marked. Woods notes that a similar pattern exists with, for example, "Go Red Sox! But I don't support the Red Sox" (2014: 5). But as Woods notes, we do *not* get a similar pattern with "Murder is wrong, but I don't disapprove of it." Expressivism predicts otherwise. It says some sentences like that should seem Moore-paradoxical. Consider an example:

(18) You have a legal obligation to pay taxes, but I don't approve of you paying taxes.

There's nothing Moore-paradoxical about (18). But if "A has a legal obligation to φ" expresses approval of A φing, there should be! My conjecture is that this problem persists no matter how we fill in the details of the expressivist's view: (18) will not seem Moore-paradoxical if we change the right-hand side by changing "approve" to "accept" or "intend," or "your paying taxes" to whatever act-description you like.

Psychological Plausibility

Expressivism explains the meaning of normative sentences in terms of the attitudes that they express, so it might seem that the view will not have any problems with psychological plausibility. If we do not *have* the relevant attitudes, the expressivist should not be explaining the meaning of our sentences in terms of those attitudes!

But other considerations can push expressivists away from offering a view that is psychologically plausible. As we saw, Toh says internal legal claims like (1) express *plural norm acceptance*. The reason for this is that Toh thinks this account of the relevant attitudes helps address a common objection to expressivism. But as Toh notes, that solution comes at some cost to the psychological plausibility of the view:

> There may be, and actually are, people, and even judges, whose legal judgments would be unaltered by their community's clear and stable adherence to contrary legal positions. We can imagine a judge whose opinion that abortion is illegal would persist even in the face of mounting judicial and societal consensus for the legality of abortion, and no real prospect of either ever changing. To think that such a judge is mistaken is one thing; but my conception of legal judgments has the seemingly implausible implication that such a judge is not even making a legal judgment (2011: 133).

Toh grants that to many this will be a counterexample, but says it is not "damning."

Regardless of whether Toh is right about that example, it is not the only case where expressivists will face pressure with respect to the psychological plausibility of their view. The expressivist needs their account of our attitudes to explain an awful lot: the semantic relations between "obligation," "permission," and negation; univocality and inconsistency; the validity of deductive inferences; why no sentences like "You have a legal obligation to pay taxes but I don't approve of your paying taxes" are Moore-paradoxical. It is unlikely a simple, familiar attitude can do all of this work. But if the expressivist appeals to some complex, exotic attitude to do this explanatory work, it will become less likely that the attitude is widely held, shared, and expressed in language.

Summing up

Expressivism does have promising features, but it also faces serious pitfalls. Is it worth the cost? That will depend, in part, on whether we can get the goodies another way. And here it is worth comparing expressivism to the view Finlay and Plunkett call *quasi-expressivism*.[64] As they put it, quasi-expressivism "agrees with expressivism that a central class of (legal or moral) statements is expressive of noncognitive attitudes or prescriptions," but disagrees with expressivism "because it diagnoses this as a feature of the pragmatics of these statements, rather than of their (purely descriptive) semantics" (2018: 50). In other words, a speaker's committed internal use of (1) pragmatically implicates that the speaker has the relevant practical attitude (e.g., norm-acceptance of your paying taxes), but this is not the literally meaning of their use of (1). Its literal meaning is still captured by a familiar truth-conditional semantics.

As a final point, it is worth reflecting on an interesting feature of Toh's proposal. Expressivists in metaethics have said little in general about flavors of deontic modality (i.e., different ordering sources like morality, prudence, law, and etiquette) and artificial normative systems in particular (like law and etiquette). As Jan Dowell (2024) notes, a sentence like "Members must not bring women to networking events" can be used in a context where it is understood relative to club rules, and "accorded no normative or action-guiding status whatsoever"; its use "seems representational, not motivational." Dowell notes that such cases seem a poor fit for an expressivist approach. But Dowell's example is close to the paradigm case for Toh's view.

---

[64] It is also noted by Kramer (2018: 403–404), Wodak (2017: 288–290), and others. It is also worth stressing once again that here I have focused on Gibbardian expressivism, but insofar as expressivist views like Yalcin's seem more promising that is partly because what they really offer is an expressivist pragmatics.

5 Are Legal Duties Made Up?

Let's turn to a final positivist theory about the meaning of "legal obligation." This fictionalist view has not been fully developed. But it has been suggested, including, at least arguably, by two pivotal figures in the history of positivism.

The first was Jeremy Bentham (1843). As Gideon Rosen notes, Bentham's "favorite case of a useful fiction" was "the notion of an obligation"; but Bentham is rarely read as a fictionalist about "legal obligation," perhaps because given Bentham's commitments about fictions, this reading yields what Rosen describes as a "*mad, mad* view" (2005: 46, 52–3). Instead, Bentham is read as holding that the literal meaning of "A is legally obligated to φ" is roughly that "A is likely to be punished if A φs." That theory has been subject to withering criticism,[65] so much so that I won't discuss it any further here.

The second figure was Hans Kelsen (1941). For Kelsen, legal normativity is a feature of normative language, which has a certain presuppositional structure. Talk of specific legal obligations in sentences like (1) presupposes the basic norm (*Grundnorm*) of the relevant jurisdiction. What is it, for Kelsen, to presuppose the basic norm? Torben Spaak notes that "on a fictionalist analysis, to presuppose the basic norm is to treat the validity (or normativity) of law as a fiction," and "having presupposed the basic norm, one can make first-order legal statements, such as 'You have a legal obligation to respect other people's property' [. . .] that are false, yet useful" (2022: 170; see also Stewart 1980).

Contemporary positivists have also suggested fictionalist views. Adam Perry offers a path to fictionalism via an account of the internal point of view. Perry treats the content of social rules—and, in turn, legal rules—as "*A*s ought to *F*" (2015: 285). Perry notes that taking the internal point of view toward this rule has certain features: it is compatible with not believing the relevant proposition; it is sensitive to practical considerations rather than evidence of the truth of the proposition; it is subject to voluntary control; and it is context-dependent (2015: 289, 292). Perry illustrates these features with the example of anarchist judges (2015: 293). They may take the internal point of view despite not believing that they ought to apply the law; they may do so because of the practical value of holding this attitude; they may have chosen to do so; and they may act as if the relevant proposition is true in some contexts

---

[65] See e.g., Hart (1982: 133–138, 141). This reading assumes that Bentham's "paraphrase" of "obligation" (in terms of a person being subject to a higher probability of sanction for action) provides its literal meaning. The "mad" alternative is to treat Bentham's "archetypation" of "obligation" (in terms of a person being physically pressed upon to prevent or force action) as its literal meaning. See Rosen (2005: 52–53).

("when making speeches, sitting on committees, and so on") but not in others (when attending "meetings of the anarchist society"). Perry then argues that these features of the internal point of view are characteristic features of the fictive attitude of *acceptance*, noting that "a connection between social rules and legal fictions is a possible, and intriguing, implication of my account" of the internal point of view (2015: 299).[66] (An aside: "acceptance" in this section should be read as a kind of cognitive attitude toward fictions that differs from belief in the respects just described, not as the non-cognitive attitude from Section 4.)

I also defended fictionalism as "first and foremost a claim about our attitudes" toward legal obligations and other instances of what is often called "merely formal normativity" (2019: 837). One further piece of evidence for this turns on how the fictive attitude of acceptance that p and the belief that p characteristically differ in how they are expressed linguistically. I believe Kim is a lawyer, so I am disposed to say "Kim is a lawyer." I accept that Atticus Finch is a lawyer, so I am also disposed to say "Atticus Finch is a lawyer." However, when I am pressed, I am disposed to qualify the latter: "But Atticus Finch isn't *really* a lawyer." Likewise, if we believe we must put the fork on the left, we are disposed to do so and say we must do so; if we accept that we must put the fork on the left, we are disposed to do so and say we must do so, but if pressed we are disposed qualify that we do not *really* have to put the fork on the left. We find a similar linguistic pattern in how claims about "legal obligations" and "legal reasons" are often qualified: "Legally, I have to φ, but I don't *really* have to φ" (Wodak 2019: 831).

Suppose this fictionalist account of our attitudes toward legal obligations is plausible. What would be the fictionalist account of the semantics of "legal obligation?"

Broadly speaking, there are two main options. Call the first *pretense fictionalism*. Compare again: "Kim is a lawyer"; "Atticus Finch is a lawyer." On this view, the first sentence is literally true and the second literally false.[67] So why utter the second sentence? Because even when the sentence is literally false, by uttering it one can assert (or otherwise convey) something about what's true

---

[66] What connection? Here Perry is uncharacteristically sloppy. Perry says "it is likely that the internal aspect of some social rules are shared fictions" (2015: 299). I think Perry means to say that some social rules are shared fictions; the internal aspect of the rule is the attitude, and the rule is (part of) its content.

[67] The issue here, to be clear, is not simply whether Atticus exists. Atticus may exist as a fictional character, an abstract rather than material entity. But consider a sentence like "Atticus weighed 160 pounds." Abstract entities do not have weights, so even if Atticus exists, the sentence is false. The same goes if we understand *being a lawyer* to be property that Atticus the abstract entity does not possess.

according to a fiction.⁶⁸ Making such an assertion can be useful even when its semantic content is false. Pretense fictionalism seems to have been Kelsen's view. Spaak claims that for Kelsen, first-order legal statements such as "You have a legal obligation to respect other people's property" are false, yet useful.⁶⁹ Toh similarly treats Kelsen's view as being that "legal assertions are best conceived as pretended or simulated normative assertions" (2018a: 73–74).

Call the second *prefix fictionalism*. On this view, "Kim is a lawyer" and "Atticus Finch is a lawyer" are both literally true. This view requires offering a different semantics for both sentences. The second sentence has an implicit fictional operator, such that its literal meaning is roughly "According to Harper Lee's novel, Atticus Finch is a lawyer." A prefix fictionalist account of the literal meaning of (1) would then be: "According to the legal fiction, you have an obligation to pay taxes because of the law."⁷⁰ When Richard Holton explored the prospects for fictionalism about sentences like (1) and (2), Holton considered prefix fictionalism: we could take such sentences to be "implicitly prefixed by something analogous to a fiction operator" (1998: 617–618).⁷¹

I think the better option to explore is pretense fictionalism (we'll see why in a moment). Here's a way to develop it. Recall the anthropologist from Section 5 who says, "Infanticide was morally permissible in Sparta." Sometimes, as Alex Worsnip writes, it is clear that speakers "intend to talk only about what is required by local standards"; but realists say that sometimes speakers also intend to talk "not about what is required by the positive local standards that are in operation 'around here', but rather by the objective, mind-independently true normative standards" (2019: 3310). On a view like Kratzer's, there is no lexical ambiguity here. The difference between the two utterances lies primarily

---

⁶⁸ I add the parenthetical qualification "or otherwise convey" as some say assertoric content is identical to semantic content; on this approach, we characterize pretense fictionalism in terms of pretend assertions.

⁶⁹ I do not think we need to interpret such first-order statements as false on Kelsen's view. (The contents of fictions can be true!) Nor does every interpreter of Kelsen claim that this is Kelsen's considered view.

⁷⁰ Interestingly, this means the formal semantics for sentences like (1) will involve stacked operators.

⁷¹ Holton argued that this proposal is more promising for (2) and for (1). Holton's reasoning is as follows. Suppose a lawyer said "My client should pay these taxes" and we asked "Do you *really* think that your client should, morally, pay these taxes?" Holton writes: "a likely reply would be: 'Who said anything about what he *morally* should do? I was just talking about his *legal* obligations. If he wants moral advice he should go to a priest.' The lawyer would object that we had misunderstood the sense of 'should' that she employing. If this is right, we have no need to make use of anything like fiction operators in understanding non-committed legal statements. Such statements do not involve the mock assertion of a normative claim; they involve the wholehearted assertion of a descriptive claim" (1998: 619). I think Holton is right, except that I think the better question is "Do you *really* think that your client should pay these taxes?" or "Do you think that your client *really* has an obligation to pay these taxes?"

in what goes in the ordering source.[72] For example, realists may say that when someone asserts (2) to talk about what is required by objective, mind-independent moral standards, (2) is true when you pay taxes in all of the worlds that are ranked best by the *objective moral reasons*.[73] The details of the realist's proposal for (2) do not really matter; what matters is that the pretense legal fictionalist can offer the same semantics for (1): e.g., (1) is true when you pay taxes in all of the worlds that are ranked best by *objective legal reasons*. If objective legal reasons do not exist, (1) is literally false (or, perhaps, truth-valueless). But the assertoric content of (1) may still be true: That according to the legal fiction such objective legal reasons exist and count in favor of tax-paying.

This is a schematic proposal; you can fill in the details for a fictionalist semantics for (1) based upon the semantics that realists offer for similar language, such as (2). And to be clear, while I endorse moral realism, this discussion does *not* presuppose that view.[74] One can be a fictionalist about (1) *and* (2); pretense moral fictionalists similarly say that "[t]he semantics offered for moral language [...] is the same semantics as that which the realist offers" (Nolan, Restall, and West 2005: 317). Instead, pretense fictionalism presupposes two points. First, the pretense fictionalist about (1) and/or (2) should offer the same semantics as realists about such discourse (while adding that the relevant sentences are often literally false or truth-valueless). Second, the pretense fictionalist about (1) or (2) takes their semantic content to come apart from their assertoric content.[75]

The fictionalist proposal is in some respects similar to moral perspectivalism: on both views, we understand "legal obligation" in terms of what's true according to a perspective. But there are three key differences. First, the relevant perspective is a fiction, not a theory. Second, we understand "legal obligation" in terms of what's true according to a perspective about *obligations* understood in a generic rather than moral sense. Third, for pretense rather than prefix fictionalists, we do not understand the literal meaning of "legal obligation" in terms of what's true according to a perspective. This last point follows from the

---

[72] I say "primarily" since, as Worsnip (2019) discusses, it may require changes to the modal base.

[73] See e.g., see Raz (1999: 29–32).

[74] Leiter holds that "Kelsen and Hart were both metaphysical anti-realists about moral norms" (2011: 671).

[75] For a discussion of this point for fictionalism in general, see Eklund (2024, esp. §4.5). To be clear, many have proposed that even for non-fictive discourse, semantic and assertoric contents systematically come apart: see especially Lewis (1980). But of course, they should not come apart *unsystematically*, for a "semantic theory without any connection between assertoric and semantic content would leave unexplained how by making an assertion, a speaker manages to convey information to others or to modify their beliefs in a more or less systematic way" (Stojnić 2017: 169).

observation that pretense moral fictionalism takes the perspective of a fiction to play a role in the *assertoric content* of a use of a sentence like (1) or (2), but not their *semantic content*: for Nolan et al., the literal meaning of (2) is exactly what the realist would take it to be, but a speaker who utters (2) thereby asserts (or otherwise conveys) a different proposition about what's true according to a fiction.[76]

You may now wonder: Why consider pretense fictionalism if it does not offer a distinct semantics for "legal obligation?" It's a good question. One answer is generated by the arguments canvassed above for taking the internal point of view to be a fictive attitude. Another answer concerns the metaphysics of legal normativity. I'll briefly sketch that now. In "The Architecture of Jurisprudence," Coleman noted that some think that law "claims to create a distinct class of reasons for acting—legal reasons" (2011: 78). Many are attracted to the more general view that a claim about what you are obligated to do is always equivalent to a claim about reasons. But claims about what you are *legally* obligated to do had better not be equivalent to claims about *moral* reasons—to take that stance is to adopt something like moral perspectivalism. Claims about what you are *legally* obligated to do had also better not be equivalent to claims about *prudential* reasons—that leads back to something like the Benthamite view that "legal obligation" means a prediction about sanctions. The natural proposal, then, is that claims about what you are legally obligated to do are equivalent to claims about *legal* reasons. So many offer sophisticated accounts that appeal at their bedrock to the notion of legal reasons (e.g., Horty 2012). But then we face the question: What on earth are legal reasons? Do legal reasons somehow compete with moral and prudential reasons in determining what you all-things-considered ought to do? Do they do so even when the legal reasons are generated by the evil laws of repressive, authoritarian legal systems?

In light of the problematic implications of taking legal reasons to be *real* reasons, it is unsurprising that David Enoch says that "legal reasons" are not "real reasons"; they are instead like "imaginary friends" (2011: 16–19). However, as Hershovitz responds: "When you say that legal reasons are not real reasons, you owe us an account of what they are, since the claim is that they are not what they purport to be" (2014: 1194: n. 55). That is exactly what fictionalism provides. If the moral realist says the meaning of (2) is explained in terms of an ordering source that consists of moral reasons for action, the fictionalist likewise says the meaning of (1) is explained in terms of an ordering source that consists of legal reasons for action. But the fictionalist can say this without any

---

[76] I'm leaving open crucial formal details about precisely what role the fictional perspective plays (for example: as a parameter in the index) in the pretense fictionalist's account of the assertoric content.

mystery—without saying that legal reasons are real reasons, and with an account of what legal reasons are given that they are not what they purport to be. That, I think, is largely what should make the fictionalist account attractive for positivists.

However, this is only a brief account of two motivations for a fictionalist approach. It is not nearly enough to explain why we should prefer fictionalism to other nearby accounts that grant that legal normativity is explained in terms of legal reasons, and take legal reasons to be in some sense *merely formally* rather than *robustly* normative.[77] The key question for any such account is whether or how it can explain the distinction between merely formal and robust normativity. Fictionalists have an answer to this. (Robust normativity is real; merely formal normativity is its fictional counterpart.) If rivals cannot explain this distinction, it seems to saddle a positivist's semantics for "legal obligation" with the commitment that there is no intelligible sense in which morality is essentially important in a way that legality is not.[78] Some will endorse that commitment, but it is at least highly contentious. It would be best for positivism, and especially the positivist's semantics, to avoid being saddled with it.

Let's turn, then, to how this view fares in relation to our five desiderata.

Scope

Fictionalism can borrow a Kratzerian semantics, and thereby inherit its theoretical virtues. Recall that for Kratzer (Section 2), "A must φ" means roughly A φs in *all* of the top-ranked worlds that are consistent with the modal base, while "A can φ" means roughly that A φs in *some* of the top-ranked worlds that are consistent with the modal base. Generalizing from this account of deontic modals provides a semantics for "obligation" and "permission." And as we saw, this enables a clear account of the meaning of sentences like (7): "People are legally, but not morally, permitted to commit adultery." And it explains the close semantic relations between "obligation" and "permission."

Univocality

For the same reason, fictionalists can offer a univocal semantics for (1) and (2), so they face no problem explaining the univocality of "obligation," and hence

---

[77] See, for example, Mitch Berman on the "Standard Positivist Picture" (2019). I thank Berman, Craig Argule, Carlos Santana, and other participants at a workshop at Penn for helpful discussion here.

[78] For example, I think the approach in Finlay and Plunkett (2018) carries that cost, though see the careful disambiguation of the relevant ways of understanding the contrast loosely drawn here in Finlay (2019).

why the term is not zeugmatic in (6). Similarly, the view does not deny the univocality of "legal," as it does not treat "legal" as if it semantically marks a fictional perspective in (1).

You may still worry about whether there is a similar issue with the assertoric rather than semantic content of mixed sentences like (6). How do we interpret what's said by the speaker if the speaker is talking about what's true according to reality *and* according to the speaker? And does "legal" mark a fictional perspective in the assertoric content of (1) and (6), such that it must also do so when it modifies "institutions" in (9)?

These are good questions. Here are two reasons to think the fictionalist faces no serious problems in answering them. First, consider analogous mixed sentences: "Kim and Atticus Finch are lawyers." There's no semantic ambiguity in this sentence, and it also does not seem that we face a serious difficulty in understanding what is being asserted.

Second, recall the above discussion of what moral realists say about the semantics of (2). Claims about "moral obligation" are not *always* made true because of facts about objective moral reasons. We saw this earlier with our anthropologist's claim about the moral permissibility of infanticide in Sparta. As Worsnip argues, the speaker's clear intentions play some role in determining when this is the case. That's why the anthropologist's claim about the moral permissibility of infanticide in Sparta turns out to be true: The speaker clearly intends to be talking about the compatibility of infanticide with *the positive morality of Spartans*, not the compatibility of infanticide with objective moral reasons. Similarly, if we grant the arguments from Perry (2015) and Wodak (2018) discussed above, the speaker's attitudes in internal legal statements of (1) play a role in determining why the relevant ordering source for what's asserted is a legal fiction. The legal fictionalist need not hold (even with respect to what's asserted) that "legal" always picks out what's true according to a legal fiction, just as the moral realist does not hold that "moral" always picks out what's true according to objective morality.

Embedding

Recall Perry's objection to moral perspectivalism, which concerns arguments like (11)–(13): "All and only persons over 18 have a legal right to vote"; "A has a legal right to vote"; "So, A is over 18." Since the literal meaning of the premises concerns what's true according to a (fallible) theory, the argument turns out to be invalid. As Perry noted (2023: 718), this is "analogous" to an objection to "some types of fictionalism" from Vision (1993). So, you may well wonder, is this also a serious problem for fictionalism?

It depends. Which types of fictionalism did Vision have in mind? Those that think sentences like "Hamlet is melancholy" are in some sense true, and so insist upon "prefixing sentences of this ilk with a phrase on the order of 'In the play Hamlet ... '" (1993: 150). Hence, prefix fictionalism has a problem with embedding. But this is not a problem for fictionalism *per se*. It is the reason I prefer pretense fictionalism. Many take the view that pretense fictionalism, as Nolan, Restall, and West noted above (2005: 317), faces no Frege-Geach-like problems with logically complex arguments.

Linguistic Data

Fictionalism avoids the problems with linguistic data that afflict the other views we considered. It does not predict that sentences like (7) are self-contradictory: "People are legally, but not morally, permitted to commit adultery." It does predict that sentences with stacked modifiers like "legal moral" in (14) are semantically anomalous. It does not predict that any sentences like (18) are Moore-paradoxical. That's all good news.

There is also some linguistic data that fictionalism is best suited to explain, like:

(19) Legally, you have to cross the street at the lights. But you don't *really* have to.

(20) Legally, you can commit adultery. But you can't *really* do that.

I noted how fictionalism explains such data above. Sentences like (19) and (20) fit a similar pattern with "Atticus Finch is a lawyer. But Atticus Finch isn't *really* a lawyer."

Psychological Plausibility

As I noted above, Perry and I argue for fictionalism by arguing that it provides a plausible account of the internal point of view in terms of the attitude of accepting a fiction. The external point of view, for the fictionalist, is the corresponding attitude of *rejecting* the legal fiction. (I won't say much about the attitude of rejecting a fiction; it should be familiar for anyone who suffered through Christopher Nolan's *Tenet*.)

But some have thought that fictionalism struggles with psychological plausibility in most contexts, and perhaps especially with law. Spaak, for example, said that Kelsen's fictionalism aspired to "mak[e] explicit what all jurists unconsciously assume in their legal thinking"; Spaak then argued that it is doubtful that all jurists *believe* that "legal validity (or normativity) as a fiction" (2022: 184). This tracks a common concern about fictionalist proposals about mathematics, modality, and other domains of inquiry: If when we make claims like (1) we're engaged in pretense, why don't we recognize this?

This objection is damning for those like Bentham and Kelsen who assume that when we engage in fiction, we know we are asserting something false. Wodak argued against that assumption in two ways (2019: 842–844). First, fictions are not always false.[79] Historical fictions are an obvious example: what's true according to the fiction is in fact often true. And historical fictions are not an exceptional case. If Arthur Conan Doyle writes "London is foggy" and "Holmes lived at 221b Baker Street," the story contains literal truths and literal falsehoods. Fictions can be false. They are not *necessarily* false. If they were, why would people read fictions to learn about the real world?[80] So if fictions are not necessarily false, accepting a fiction and engaging in pretense cannot be understood as knowingly asserting falsehoods. This point is especially helpful for the legal fictionalist if we understand the content of the relevant fiction such that it can be true. If a fiction about legal reasons for action is a fiction about reasons which can be real, but need not be real,[81] then accepting that fiction will involve accepting propositions which are true according to the fiction and sometimes literally true.

Second, we can get swept up in fictions without recognizing that this is the case. Just as we can believe p without believing that we believe p, we can fictively accept p without believing that we fictively accept p. Opacity of mind is common (see Carruthers 2011). To know whether our attitudes in a domain of inquiry are fictive requires theoretical reflection (Joyce 2001: 292). Many of us do not ask whether our attitudes in a domain bear the distinct markers of fictive acceptance that were briefly discussed above. And if we did ask, the answer may not be obvious in cases where we take p to be true and true-according-to-a-fiction; it's harder to tell whether you have the attitude of accepting that London is foggy when you happen to independently believe that London is foggy.

Summing up

Again, a fictionalist approach to the semantics of "legal obligation" is far less developed than its rivals. But given how much the view can borrow from the

---

[79] Perry unfortunately suggests this stance since Perry characterizes fictive acceptance as an attitude "held towards a false proposition," and a "legal fiction" as "a legal presumption of a proposition that is false" (2015: 299). But this is hard to square with Perry's discussion of how we can believe and accept p (290–291).

[80] For an overview of the philosophical literature on this phenomenon, see Currie et al (2023).

[81] See Wodak (2019) for related discussion of how such a story might be developed.

semantic views offered by others, fictionalism can stick closely to a promising Kratzerian approach (Section 2), while offering a promising account of the ways in which claims like (1) and (2) seem both similar and different. They can receive an identical semantic treatment, so for moral realists the relevant uses of (2) are true when tax-paying is supported by moral reasons, and for legal fictionalists (1) is true when tax-paying is supported by legal reasons. But they are different insofar as those legal reasons need not be real.

6 Hume's Law and the Law

Hume's Law is often glossed as follows: one cannot derive an "ought" from an "is." What Hume actually said is more verbose and open to interpretation:

> In every system of morality, which I have hitherto met with, I have always remark'd, that the author proceeds for some time in the ordinary way of reasoning, and establishes the being of a God, or makes observations concerning human affairs; when of a sudden I am surpriz'd to find, that instead of the usual copulations of propositions, is, and is not, I meet with no proposition that is not connected with an ought, or an ought not. This change is imperceptible; but is, however, of the last consequence. For as this ought, or ought not, expresses some new relation or affirmation, 'tis necessary that it should be observ'd and explain'd; and at the same time that a reason should be given, for what seems altogether inconceivable, how this new relation can be a deduction from others, which are entirely different from it (1896: 469).

Regardless of whether it is what Hume meant by these remarks, Hume's Law is often treated as a logical thesis. And while the thesis is arguably subject to counterexamples, it is widely thought to have profound significance for philosophy of law.

Indeed, antipositivists have long said that legal prescriptivity is a problem for positivism because positivism violates Hume's Law. Finnis claims that "'ought' is never derivable from 'is',," and positivism "fails to meet this demand of logic coherently" (2002: 4). Hershovitz, more modestly, holds that Hart's version of positivism "seems to license inferences that run afoul of David Hume's famous injunction that you cannot derive an ought from an is," and "anyone who would defend a legal positivism like Hart's must show Hume wrong or navigate around his injunction that you cannot derive an ought from an is" (2014: 1168). Positivists tend to agree with this more modest assessment, but insist that positivism can successfully "navigate around" Hume's Law.

Indeed, the compatibility of positivism with Hume's Law has become one of the major "dialectical tributaries" in contemporary philosophy of law, and in many respects it is a "Kelsenian tributary" (Toh 2018b: 17). Kelsen's discussion of positivism and Hume's Law has proved to be enormously influential on current work.[82] It is a major theme in Shapiro's *Legality*. Shapiro writes that positivism "appears to violate the famous principle introduced by David Hume [...], which states that one can never derive an ought from an is," and that positivists need to meet this "extremely serious challenge" (2011: 47). Shapiro calls it Hume's Challenge. As Toh notes, Shapiro's "exposition" of the challenge "essentially replicates" Kelsen's presentation of the problem (2018b: 18). It is also similar, I'd add, to the presentation of the problem in Raz (1999: 145–155).

The three positivist theories that we considered in Sections 3 to 5 offer different ways of navigating around Hume's Law, and thereby answering the challenge. For moral perspectivalists, the answer is that sentences like (1), when true, do not correspond to *normative* facts. Moral perspectivalists say that (1) means "According to the legal point of view, you have a moral obligation to pay taxes." As such, (1) uses a normative (and indeed moral) concept, OBLIGATION,[83] but is still a descriptive claim. As Shapiro writes, "'legal statements' like (1) are descriptive ... because they describe the moral perspective of the law" (2011: 191). True descriptive propositions about the moral perspective of the law can be entailed by descriptive propositions alone without violating Hume's Law. So there is no "ought" from "is," but only an "is from an is" (2011: 188).

Expressivists, including Toh, are also concerned about Hume's Challenge. Toh says that "a normative statement (insofar as it has or requires further grounds) must have normative grounds in addition to any factual ones." Why? Because of

> the existence of an inferential gap between normative statements on the one hand and factual statements on the other. This is the so-called *is-ought* gap, supposedly argued for by Hume, according to which no *ought*-statement can be derived from a consistent set of *is*-statements alone (2008: 469).

Toh goes on to claim that the Hume's Law means that "any justification or defense of a normative statement—e.g., an internal legal statement—would have to appeal to at least one normative premise," which makes one prominent formulation of positivism (the "social fact thesis") "untenable" (2008: 469–470). Toh's expressivist answer to the challenge is to separate internal from external legal statements. When (1) is an internal legal statement, it is not truth-apt, so there is no fact about obligations. As such, there is no "ought" fact that is derived from an "is." When (2) is an external legal statement, it is truth-apt, but

---

[82] See, among others, Green (1999: 35–36); Marmor (2009: 158–159; 2010: 17); Marmor and Sarch (2019: §2.1.2); Raz (1981: 456; 1999: 154–155, 170–177; see also 2009); Bix (2006: 7; 2015: 129–131); Gragl (2017); Demiray (2015); Rosati (2016: 310); Coleman and Leiter (2010: 244). See also Raz (1999:), Green and Adams (2019: §2), and Marmor and Sarch (2019: §2.1.2).

[83] I use the lower case for the concept OBLIGATION, as distinct from the word "obligation."

it is not a normative claim. It is a descriptive claim. Here the expressivist seems to hold that when (1) is an internal legal statement, it uses a different, descriptive concept of OBLIGATION. (Recall that the expressivist is committed to treating claims like (1) as ambiguous.) Hence, neither internal nor external legal statements turn out to derive an "ought" from an "is." (See Toh [2018: 11] for a more careful discussion of this.)

Fictionalists can also avoid deriving an "ought" from an "is" in one of two ways. The prefix fictionalist mirrors the perspectivalist strategy: (1) turns out to be a literally true descriptive proposition about what is true according to a point of view. The pretense fictionalist, by contrast, can take (1) to be truth-apt but literally false. If (1) is either a true descriptive proposition or a false normative proposition, then either way fictionalists can hold that no "ought" fact is derived from an "is" fact alone.

Any of these semantic strategies, then, offers a way of navigating around Hume's Law. But Chilovi and Wodak (2021) argued that in this respect, none of these strategies solve a genuine problem, but instead solve a pseudo-problem. The widespread assumption that Hume's Law has profound significance for theories of nature of law is mistaken.

There are two ways of seeing why this assumption is mistaken. The first is relatively quick. It turns on noting that Hume's Law is, as Gillian Russell calls it, a *barrier to entailment*: "something that gets in the way of there being valid arguments from premises of one kind to conclusions of another" (2023: 1). As Russell discusses at length, Hume's Law is one of several barriers to entailment. The "other barrier theses are so uncontroversial as to be platitudes, including the following (2023: 1–2):

> The past/future barrier: no claims about the future from claims about the past
> The particular/universal barrier: no universal claims from particular ones
> The indexical barrier: no indexical claims from claims which are not indexical.

Russell notes that many have thought that Hume's Law has profound significance for how we think about moral claims like (2), but this view has largely been abandoned. The corresponding view that Hume's Law has profound significance for how we think about legal claims like (1), however, remains prominent (Russell 2023: 2, fn. 2). But let's stick to the moral case. Many thought that because of Hume's Law, we must adopt some novel metaphysical, semantic, or epistemological thesis, such as holding that "there are no moral truths—only non-assertoric, expressive moral speech acts, which perhaps rather command, or express attitudes" (2023: 15). Russell makes short work of this, arguing that "if Hume's Law is just one among several barriers, we can ask what we would make of such a conclusion in other cases," such as "the past/future barrier" or "the particular/universal barrier." Clearly, we need not accept any novel metaphysics, semantics, or epistemology to navigate these barriers to implication. We need not say that "when someone utters 'the sun will rise tomorrow' they merely express a wish this be so, or they are commanding the sun to rise," or be "expressivists about the Universal" (2023: 15). So if barriers to entailment do not *generally* have such significant implications, why does Hume's Law have profound significance for morality? Or law?

The longer, more scenic route to see why the assumption is mistaken requires carefully distinguishing the contents of Hume's Law and positivism. If we gloss Hume's Law and positivism quickly and carelessly, they look incompatible. The former says one cannot derive an "ought" from an "is," while the latter derives an "ought" from an "is!" But this only generates an incompatibility if we equivocate on the meaning of "derive." Hume's Law is a logical thesis—the relevant notion of "derivation" is *entailment*. Positivism is a metaphysical thesis. There is some dispute about how it should be formulated, but the relevant notion of "derivation" may be something like *grounding* or *real definition*. The details don't matter; any such metaphysical relation differs from entailment. So Hume's Law says, roughly, that no sentence or proposition of the form "You are legally obligated to pay taxes" is *entailed* by a set of descriptive propositions alone. But contrast, positivism says, roughly, that all facts like [You are legally obligated to pay taxes] are fully grounded in descriptive social facts.[84] Stated more carefully, there is no inconsistency between Hume's Law and positivism, taken on their own.

You might think this point hinges on idiosyncratic formulations of Hume's Law and positivism. But Shapiro (2011) agrees that Hume's Law is a logical thesis, and positivism is a thesis about grounding. And as we saw above, Toh (2008) moves quickly between positivism as a claim about what grounds legal facts and Hume's Law as an inferential gap between statements. Finnis (2002) said Hume's Law is a "demand of logic"; no one thinks positivism is also a putative logical thesis. So everyone agrees that there is some gap between formulations of Hume's Law and positivism. And there had better be *some* gap between the two. Suppose Hume's Law were instead interpreted as (say) the universally quantified metaphysical thesis that no fact of the form [You ought to φ] is fully grounded in descriptive facts alone. If this were the case, then appealing to Hume's Law to undermine positivism would amount to appealing to a universally quantified, highly tendentious metaphysical thesis to undermine a far more modest and appealing metaphysical thesis (Chilovi and Wodak 2021: 635, 648–649).

---

[84] I use square brackets to distinguish the fact that [*p*] from the sentence or proposition "*p*."

It seems, then, that Hume's Law cannot itself be inconsistent with positivism. There must be a gap between the two. So in order for Hume's Law to be incompatible with positivism, some further commitments must bridge that gap. Put less metaphorically: one would need to subscribe to further commitments that connect the two relevant notions of derivation, such that if "q" does not entail "p," then [p] is not fully grounded in [q]. As Samuele Chilovi and I argue, there's just no good way to bridge that gap.

Consider, for example, how Shapiro frames Hume's Challenge (2011: 43):

> According to the legal positivist, the content of the law is ultimately determined by social facts alone. To know the law, therefore, one must (at least in principle) be able to derive this information exclusively from knowledge of social facts. But knowledge of the law is normative whereas knowledge of social facts is descriptive. How can normative knowledge be derived exclusively from descriptive knowledge? That would be to derive facts about what one legally ought to do from judgments about what is the case. Legal positivism, therefore, appears to violate the famous principle introduced by David Hume (often called Hume's Law), which states that one can never derive an ought from an is.

This passage seems to rely on two bridge principles. One is needed to justify the inference from the first sentence to the second in the passage above: if [p] fully grounded in [q], then one can at least in principle derive knowledge of p exclusively from knowledge of q. Hence, if the content of the law is ultimately determined by social facts alone, then one can at least in principle derive knowledge of the content of the law p exclusively from knowledge of social facts. There are many counterexamples to this general principle linking grounding to knowledge. Most involve cases where it is *opaque* that [p] fully grounded in [q]: e.g., that facts about water are fully grounded in facts about H_2O. Plausibly, one cannot derive knowledge of water exclusively from knowledge of H_2O, without knowing the relevant relation between water and H_2O.

The second bridge principle is needed to justify the inference in the second half of the passage above: that if "normative knowledge [can] be derived exclusively from descriptive knowledge," then Hume's Law is violated. The general principle seems to be that if "q" does not entail "p," one cannot in principle derive knowledge of p from knowledge of q. Shapiro seems to endorse this principle in full generality:

> Because normative conclusions cannot be derived exclusively from descriptive premises, normative reasoners must conform to a certain pattern of inference: they must ensure that their reasoning takes a normative judgment as input if a normative judgment is the output. Call this "normative in, normative out" pattern of inference a "NINO" pattern. Hume's Law is violated,

therefore, if a normative judgment comes out but only descriptive judgments went in. Call this offending sequence a "DINO" pattern.

> The worry about legal positivism [...] is that it violates Hume's Law by licensing DINO patterns of inference. [...] Call this objection to legal positivism "Hume's Challenge" (2011: 48).

The assumption again seems to be that reasoners must conform to deductively valid patterns of inference: if "q" does not entail "p," one cannot infer p from q.

This second bridge principle generates untenable skepticism in two ways. The first returns to Russell's point that Hume's Law is just one of several barriers to entailment; there are similar barriers between the past and the future and the particular and the universal. Suppose we grant that if "q" does not entail "p," one cannot infer p from q. If no set of sentences or propositions about the past entails anything about the future, then it seems that we cannot infer anything about the future from knowledge of the past: We cannot infer the conclusion that the sun will rise tomorrow from any set of premises about how often the sun has risen in the past. That is: if a "DINO" pattern of inference is objectionable, then so is a "past in, future out" pattern of inference—i.e., so is induction!

Some may bite this bullet. Perhaps the conclusion that the sun will rise tomorrow can (only) be inferred from premises that include propositions about the future—that is, based on some deductively valid "future in, future out" pattern of inference. If a good deductive argument for that conclusion is available, believing that the sun will rise tomorrow is *propositionally justified*. But for your actual belief that the sun will rise tomorrow to be *doxastically justified*, and hence for it to be possible for you to *know* this conclusion, your belief that the sun will rise tomorrow must be based on that kosher "future in, future out" pattern of inference. But is it? Gilbert Harman (1984) famously argued that human reasoning is rarely deductively valid. It seems plausible that most of us actually rely on inductive "past in, future out" reasoning. Many have similarly argued that sophisticated legal reasoning is rarely deductively valid.[85] If we can only infer q from premises that entail q, then laypeople and lawyers alike rarely gain inferential knowledge. The conclusions that we infer are rarely entailed by our premises, so our inferences are based on verboten patterns of inference.

That was the scenic route. The general lesson is how hard it is to see how to bridge the gap between Hume's law and positivism. Any way of doing so will require bridge principles to connect logical entailment to metaphysical grounding (or whatever non-logical relation one uses to formulate positivism). Those bridge principles will be contentious and will generate undesirable

---

[85] See Horty (2004, 2011), Holmes, Jr. (1881), and Pound (1912: 464).

commitments about analogous barriers to entailment between the past and future and the particular and the universal.

If Chilovi and I are right, then even Hershovitz's modest assessment is a mistake. It is false that anyone who would defend legal positivism must show Hume wrong or navigate around Hume's injunction that you cannot derive an ought from an is. Instead, they can accept that legal facts (including prescriptive legal facts) can be fully grounded in descriptive social facts alone, and accept that prescriptive legal statements or propositions cannot be entailed by descriptive social propositions alone. These are compatible as long as [p] can be fully grounded in [q] even if "q" does not entail "p."

This may seem like something of an odd way to wrap up the present project. The main impetus for positivists to develop theories of the semantics of "legal obligation" has been the Kelsenian tributary that positivism appears to derive legal obligations from descriptive social facts alone, and thereby violate Hume's Law. But this tributary, it seems, should dry up. Should we still care about the semantics of "legal obligation?"

I think so, at least for those engaged in the project of general jurisprudence—that is, of explaining how legal thought and talk fit into reality overall. One component of that project is to explain the semantics of legal thought and talk (Plunkett and Shapiro 2017: 54). As we saw from the start, legal prescriptivity is central to legal thought and talk. So there are good reasons to find the semantics of legal prescriptivity interesting even if it turns out to have little significance for the prospects of positivism and antipositivism.

In this respect, it is worth noting one final reason the prescriptivity of legal language poses no clear threat to positivism. Leading anti-positivists like Mark Greenberg still object that "legal positivists have struggled to explain the use of the term *legal obligation*" (2013: 1304). There are many reasons why positivists like Raz and Shapiro have struggled to do so; but many of the problems they face, such as in accommodating linguistic data, also apply to the most natural semantic theories available to anti-positivism. When this has been pointed out, no solution has been offered; instead, anti-positivists have expressed nonchalance about linguistic data.[86] How, then, can it be objectionable for positivists to struggle to explain the use of *legal obligation* but not for anti-positivists to struggle to explain the use of that same term? The problem of explaining the use of *legal obligation*, it seems, is, if anything, a problem for everyone.

---

[86] See especially Hershovitz's response to Wodak (2018): "I'm not sure how much weight we should place on linguistic intuitions ..., since they may reflect confusions about the underlying subject matter or embed shortcuts that allow us to communicate efficiently. All this is a bit beside the point, ... since my claim isn't about (or dependent on) the way we use words. It's a claim about the nature of practical normativity and law's place within it" (2023: 231, fn. 53).

7 Conclusion

I started this project with the wise words of John Gardner (2012: 133):

> The place to begin, nobody doubts, is with the language that law-applying officials use. In explaining the law, they cannot but use the language of obligations, rights, permissions, powers, liabilities and so on. What they thereby claim – and they cannot say it without claiming it – is that the law imposes obligations, creates rights, grants permissions, confers powers, gives rise to liabilities, and so on. The question is: What do these claims amount to?

The place to end is to see whether we have made progress in answering that question.

My main goal has not been to defend a single answer—though I am highly sympathetic to fictionalism. Instead, my main goal has been to clarify the question itself and the range of theories on offer for the meaning of "legal obligation." I'll end by reviewing three overarching lessons from our discussion.

First, we need to distinguish the task of providing an account of the semantics for "legal obligation" from nearby tasks with which it is easily conflated. An account of the locutionary act of uttering "You have a legal obligation to pay taxes" differs from an account of the illocutionary act thereby performed. An account of the literal meaning of the utterance is different from an account of what it pragmatically implicates.

Second, we need to subject accounts of the semantics for "legal obligation" to scrutiny using the standard tools and considerations from philosophy of language and linguistics. This includes: not focusing narrowly on "obligations," but broadly on related terms (including "rights, permissions, powers, liabilities, and so on"); explaining the univocality of terms like "obligation" and "legal," while predicting ambiguity only when this is supported by linguistic data; explaining what "You have a legal obligation to pay taxes" means when it is embedded; testing theories for whether they explain the relevant linguistic data; and considering each theory's psychological plausibility.

Third, the substantive theories offered by philosophers of law have been too quick to depart from a simple way to generalize the textbook Kratzerian approach to the semantics of deontic modals. Given the relative virtues of that approach, departing from it requires significant justification. But instead, philosophers of law who depart from this textbook semantics neglect to engage with it almost entirely.

These lessons leave us with plenty more to learn about the language of law. My hope is that they also put us on a better path to shed more light than heat on the topic.

References

Ásgeirsson, H. (2020). The Nature and Value of Vagueness in the Law. Oxford University Press.

Atiq, E. H. (2025). Contemporary non-positivism. Elements in Philosophy of Law. https://www.cambridge.org/core/elements/abs/contemporary-nonpositivism/E45EB0EC5BA59FE7D7D36F7C95A707EC

Austin, J. L. (1975). How to Do Things With Words. Cambridge:: Harvard University Press.

Bentham, J. (1843). The works of Jeremy Bentham. In J. Bowring (ed.). Edinburgh: William Tait.

Berman, M. N. (2019). Of law and other artificial normative systems. In K. Toh, D. Plunkett, and S. Shapiro (eds.), Dimensions of Normativity: New Essays on Metaethics and Jurisprudence, 137–164. and Oxford University Press: New York.

Bix, B. (2006). Legal positivism and "explaining" normativity and authority. American Philosophical Association Newsletter on Philosophy and Law, 5(2), 09–05.

Bix, B. H. (2015). Rules and normativity in law. In M. Araszkiewicz, P. Banaś, T. Gizbert-Studnicki, and K. Płeszka (eds.), Problems of Normativity, Rules and Rule-Following, 125–146. Springer.

Bulygin, E. (2015). Norms, normative propositions and legal statements (1982). In C. Bernal, C. Huerta, T. Mazzarese et al. (eds.), Essays in Legal Philosophy. Oxford: Oxford University Press, 188–206.

Carruthers, P. (2011). The Opacity of Mind: An Integrative Theory of Self-Knowledge. Oxford: Oxford University Press.

Chilovi, S., & Wodak, D. (2021). On the (in) significance of Hume's Law. Philosophical Studies, 179(2), 633–653.

Coleman, J. L. (2011). The architecture of jurisprudence. Yale Law Yournal, 121(1), 2–80.

Coleman, J. L., & Leiter, B. (2010). Legal positivism. In Dennis Patterson (ed.), A Companion to Philosophy of Law and Legal Theory, 228–248 (2nd ed.). Wiley-Blackwell.

Coleman, J. L. (2007). Beyond the Separability Thesis: Moral Semantics and the Methodology of Jurisprudence. Oxford Journal of Legal Studies, 27(4), 581–608, https://doi.org/10.1093/ojls/gqm014.

Cover, R. (1975). Justice Accused: Antislavery and the Judicial Process. New Haven: Yale University Press.

Currie, A. (2020). Obligation and modality (Doctoral dissertation, University of Oxford).

Currie, G., Ferguson, H., Frascaroli, J. et al. (2023). Learning from Fiction 1. In The Routledge Handbook of Fiction and Belief (pp. 126–138). New York: Routledge.

Demiray, M. R. (2015). Natural law theory, legal positivism, and the normativity of law. The European Legacy, 20(8), 807–826.

Dindjer, H. (2020). The new legal anti-positivism. Legal Theory, 26(3), 181–213.

Dowell, J. (2016). Review of *confusion of tongues*. Mind, 125, 585–593.

Dowell, J. (2020). Finlay's methodology: Synthetic, not analytic. Analysis, 80(1), 562–566.

Dowell, J. (2024). Semantics for deontic modals. In E. Lepore & U. Stojnic (eds.), Oxford Handbook of Contemporary Philosophy of Language, 476–504. Oxford: Oxford University Press.

Eklund, M. (2024). Fictionalism. In Edward N. Zalta & U. Nodelman (eds.), The Stanford Encyclopedia of Philosophy (Spring 2024 Edition), https://plato.stanford.edu/archives/spr2024/entries/fictionalism/.

Endicott, T. (2022). Law and language. In Edward N. Zalta (ed.), The Stanford Encyclopedia of Philosophy (Spring 2022 Edition), https://plato.stanford.edu/archives/spr2022/entries/law-language/.

Enoch, D. (2011). Reason-giving and the law. Oxford Studies in the Philosophy of Law, 1, 1–38.

Enoch, D., & Toh, K. (2013). Legal as a thick concept. In W. Waluchow and S. Sciaraffa (eds.), Philosophical Foundations of the Nature of Law, 257–278. Oxford: Oxford Academic.

Etchemendy, M. X. (2016). New directions in legal expressivism. Legal Theory, 22(1), 1–21.

Falkum, I. L., & Vicente, A. (2015). Polysemy: Current Perspectives and Approaches. Lingua, 157, 1–16.

Finlay, S. (2014). Confusion of Tongues: A Theory of Normative Language. New York: Oxford University Press.

Finlay, S. (2019). Defining normativity. In in David Plunkett, Scott J. Shapiro, and Kevin Toh (eds.), Dimensions of Normativity: New Essays on Metaethics and Jurisprudence, 187–220. New York: Oxford University Press.

Finlay, S., & Plunkett, D. (2018). Quasi-expressivism about statements of law: A Hartian theory. Oxford Studies in Philosophy of Law, 3, 49–86.

Finnis, J. (2002). Natural law: The classical theory. In Coleman, J. L., & Shapiro, S. (eds.), The Oxford Handbook of Jurisprudence & Philosophy of Law, 1–103. New York: Oxford University Press.

Gardner, J. (2012). Law as a Leap of Faith: Essays on Law in General. Oxford: Oxford University Press.

Geach, P. T. (1958). Imperative and deontic logic. Analysis, 18(3), 49–56.

Gibbard, A. (1990). Wise Choices, Apt Feelings: A Theory of Normative Judgment. Cambridge: Harvard University Press.

Gragl, P. (2017). In defence of Kelsenian monism: Countering Hart and Raz. Jurisprudence, 8(2), 287–318.

Green, L. (1999). Positivism and conventionalism. Canadian Journal of Law & Jurisprudence, 12(1), 35–52.

Green, L. (2002). Law and obligation. In J. L. Coleman, K. E. Himma and S. J. Shapiro (eds.), The Oxford Handbook of Jurisprudence and Philosophy of Law (pp. 514–547). Oxford: Oxford University Press.

Green, L., & Adams, T. (2019). Legal positivism. In Edward N. Zalta (ed.), The Stanford Encyclopedia of Philosophy (Winter 2019 Edition), https://plato.stanford.edu/archives/win2019/entries/legal-positivism/.

Greenberg, M. (2011). The standard picture and its discontents. Oxford Studies in the Philosophy of Law, 1, 39–106.

Greenberg, M. (2013). The moral impact theory of law. Yale Law Journal, 123, 1288.

Harman, G. (1984). Logic and reasoning. Synthese, 60(1), 107–127.

Hart, H. L. A. (1949). The Ascription of Responsibility and Rights. Proceedings of the Aristotelian Society, 49, 171–194.

Hart, H. L. A. (1983). Essays in Jurisprudence and Philosophy. Oxford: Oxford University Press.

Hart, H. L. A. (1982). Essays on Bentham: Jurisprudence and Political Philosophy. Oxford: Oxford University Press.

Hart, H. L. A. (2012). The Concept of Law. Oxford: Oxford University Press.

Heim, I. & Kratzer, A. (1998). Semantics in Generative Grammar. Malden: Wiley-Blackwell

Hershovitz, S. (2014). The end of jurisprudence. Yale Law Journal, 124, 1160.

Hershovitz, S. (2014). The end of jurisprudence. Yale Law Journal, 124, 1160.

Hershovitz, S. (2023). Law is a Moral Practice. Cambridge: Harvard University Press.

Holmes, Jr., O. W. (1881). The Common Law. Boston: Little, Brown.

Holton, R. (1998). Positivism and the internal point of view. Law and Philosophy 17(5/6), 597–625.

Horty J. F. (2004). The Result Model of Precedent. Legal Theory, 10(1), 19-31. doi:10.1017/S1352325204000151.

Horty, J. (2014). Deontic modals: Why abandon the classical semantics? Pacific Philosophical Quarterly, 95, 424–460.

Horty, J. F. (2011). Rules and reasons in the theory of precedent. Legal Theory, 17(1), 1–33.

Horty, J. F. (2012). Reasons as Defaults. Oxford University Press.

Hume, D. (1896). A Treatise of Human Nature. Oxford: Clarendon Press.

Kelsen, H. (1941). The pure theory of law and analytical jurisprudence. Harvard Law Review, 55, 44.

Kratzer, A. (1991). Modality. In A. von Stechow and D. Wunderlich (eds.), Semantics: An International Handbook of Contemporary Research (pp. 639–50). Berlin: de Gruyter.

Kratzer, A. (1997). What 'Must' and 'Can' Must and Can Mean. Linguistics and Philosophy, 1(3), 337–355.

Kramer, M. H. (2018). Hart and the metaphysics and semantics of legal normativity. Ratio Juris, 31(4), 396–420.

Incurvati, L., & Schlöder, J. J. (2021). Inferential expressivism and the negation problem. Oxford Studies in Metaethics, 16, 80–107.

Joyce, R. (2001). The myth of morality. Cambridge: Cambridge University Press.

Leiter, B. (2011). The demarcation problem in jurisprudence: A new case for scepticism. Oxford Journal of Legal Studies, 31(4), 663–677.

Lewis, D. K. (1980). Index, context and content. In S. Kanger and S. Öhman (eds.), Philosophy and Grammar (pp. 79–100). Dordrecht: Reidel. Reprinted in D. K. Lewis (1997). Papers in Philosophical Logic Vol. 1, 21–44. Cambridge: Cambridge University Press.

Liu, M. (2024). How to think about zeugmatic oddness. Review of Philosophy and Psychology, 15 (4), 1109–1132.

Marmor, A. (2009). Social Conventions: From Language to Law. Princeton: Princeton University Press.

Marmor, A. (2010). Philosophy of Law. Princeton: Princeton University Press.

Marmor, A., & Sarch, A. (2019). The nature of law. In Zalta, E. N. (ed.), The Stanford encyclopedia of Philosophy. https://plato.stanford.edu/archives/fall2019/entries/lawphil-nature.

Matthewson, L. (2004). On the methodology of semantic fieldwork. International Journal of American Linguistics, 70(4), 369–415.

Matthewson, L. (2016). Modality. In M. Aloni and P. Dekker (eds.), Cambridge Handbook of Formal Semantics (pp. 525–559), Cambridge: Cambridge University Press.

Nolan, D., Restall, G., & West, C. (2005). Moral fictionalism versus the rest. Australasian Journal of Philosophy, 83(3), 307–330.

Perry, A. (2015). The internal aspect of social rules. Oxford Journal of Legal Studies, 35(2), 283–300.

Perry, A. (2023). According to law. Analysis, 83(4), 717–722.
Plunkett, D., & Shapiro, S. (2017). Law, morality, and everything else: General jurisprudence as a branch of metanormative inquiry. Ethics, 128(1), 37–68.
Plunkett, D., & Wodak, D. (2022a). The disunity of legal reality. Legal Theory, 28(3), 235–267.
Plunkett, D., & Wodak, D. (2022b). Legal positivism and the real definition of law. Jurisprudence, 13(3), 317–348.
Pound, R. (1912). The scope and purpose of sociological jurisprudence. Harvard Law Review, 25, 489–516.
Prior, A. (1960). The autonomy of ethics. Australasian Journal of Philosophy, 38(3), 199–206.
Raz, J. (1981). The purity of the pure theory. Revue Internationale de Philosophie, 35(138), 441–459.
Raz, J. (1984). Hart on Moral and Legal Duties. Oxford Journal of Legal Studies, 4(1), 123–131.
Raz, J. (1999). Practical reason and norms. Oxford: Oxford University Press.
Raz, J. (2009). The Authority of Law: Essays on Law and Morality (2nd ed.). New York: Oxford University Press.
Rosati, C. (2016). Normativity and the planning theory of law. Jurisprudence, 7(2), 307–324.
Rosen, G. (2005). Problems in the History of Fictionalism. In M. E. Kalderon (ed.), Fictionalism in Metaphysics (pp. 14–64). Oxford University Press.
Russell, G. K. (2023). Barriers to Entailment: Hume's Law and Other Limits on Logical Consequence. New York: Oxford University Press.
Ryu, A., and Sewell, T. (forthcoming). Taking the legal perspective seriously. Analysis. https://doi.org/10.1093/analys/anae037.
Santana, C. (2020). How we can make good use of linguistic intuitions, even if they are not good evidence. . In S., Schindler, A. Drożdżowicz, and K. Brøcker (eds.), Linguistic Intuitions: Evidence and Method, 129–148. Oxford: Oxford University Press.
Schaus, S. (2014). How to think about law as morality: A comment on Greenberg and Hershovitz. Yale Law Journal Forum, 124, 224.
Schroeder, M. (2008). Being For: Evaluating the Semantic Program of Expressivism. Oxford: Oxford University Press.
Sennet, A. (2021). Ambiguity. In E. N. Zalta (ed.), The Stanford Encyclopedia of Philosophy, https://plato.stanford.edu/archives/spr2016/entries/ambiguity/.
Shapiro, S. J. (2006). What is the internal point of view. Fordham Law Review, 75, 1157.
Shapiro, S. (2011). Legality. Harvard University Press.

References

Silk, A. (2014). Why "ought" detaches: Or, why you ought to get with my friends (if you want to be my lover). Philosophers' Imprint, 14 (7), 1–16.

Silk, A. (2019). Normativity in Language and Law. In K. Toh, D. Plunkett and S. Shapiro (eds.), Dimensions of Normativity: New Essays on Metaethics and Jurisprudence, 287–313. New York: Oxford University Press.

Spaak, T. (2022). Kelsen's metaethics. Ratio Juris, 35(2), 158–190.

Stewart, I. (1980). The basic norm as fiction. Juridical Review, 20, 199–224.

Stojnić, U. (2017). On the connection between semantic content and the objects of assertion. Philosophical Topics, 45(2), 163–180.

Streumer, B., & Wodak, D. (2021). Why formal objections to the error theory fail. Analysis, 81(2), 254–262.

Streumer, B., & Wodak, D. (2023). Do formal objections to the error theory overgeneralize? Analysis, 83(4), 732–741. https://doi.org/10.1093/analys/anad034.

Streumer, B., & Wodak, D. (2023). Do formal objections to the error theory overgeneralize? Analysis, 83(4), 732–741.

Thomson, J. J. (2008). Normativity. Chicago: Open Court Press.

Toh, K. (2005). Hart's expressivism and his Benthamite project. Legal Theory, 11(2), 75–123.

Toh, K. (2007). Raz on detachment, acceptance, and describability. Oxford Journal of Legal Studies, 27(3), 403–427.

Toh, K. (2008). An argument against the social fact thesis (and some additional preliminary steps towards a new conception of legal positivism). Law and Philosophy, 27(5), 445–504.

Toh, K. (2011). Legal judgments as plural acceptances of norms. In L. Green and B. Leiter (eds), Oxford Studies in the Philosophy of Law, 107–137. Oxford: Oxford University Press.

Toh, K. (2013). Jurisprudential theories and first-order legal judgments. Philosophy Compass, 8(5), 457–471.

Toh, K. (2018a). Law, Morality, Art, the Works. In Luka B., K. Einar Himma, and C. Roversi (eds.), Law as an Artifact. Oxford Academic. https://doi.org/10.1093/oso/9780198821977.003.0004.

Toh, K. (2018b). Plan-attitudes, plan-contents, and bootstrapping: Some thoughts on the planning theory of law. In J. Gardner, L. Green, and B. Leiter (eds.), Oxford studies in philosophy of law. (Vol. 3). Oxford: Oxford University.

Rosen, G. (2005). Problems in the History of Fictionalism. In M. E. Kalderon (ed.), Fictionalism in Metaphysics (pp. 14–64). Oxford University Press.

Viebahn, E., & Vetter, B. (2016). How many meanings for "may"? The case for modal polysemy. Philosopher's Imprint, 16(10), 1–26.

Vision, G. (1993). Fiction and Fictionalist Reductions. Pacific Philosophical Quarterly, 74, 150–174.

Von Wright, G. H. (1981). On the logic of norms and actions. In New Studies in Deontic Logic: Norms, Actions, and the Foundations of Ethics (pp. 3–35). Dordrecht: Springer Netherlands.

Wodak, D. (2017). Expressivism and varieties of normativity. Oxford Studies in Metaethics, 12(12), 1–37.

Wodak, D. (2018). What does "legal obligation" mean? Pacific Philosophical Quarterly, 99(4), 790–816.

Wodak, D. (2019). Mere formalities: Fictional normativity and normative authority. Canadian Journal of Philosophy, 49(6), 828–850.

Wodak, D. (2021). Hrafn Asgeirsson, the nature and value of vagueness in law. Ethics, 131(4), 777–781.

Woods, J. (2014). Expressivism and Moore's Paradox. Philosophers' Imprint, 14, 1–12.

Worsnip, A. (2019). "Ought"-contextualism beyond the parochial. Philosophical Studies, 176, 3099–3119.

Yalcin, Seth. (2012). Bayesian Expressivism. Proceedings of the Aristotelian Society, 112, 123–160.

Philosophy of Law

Series Editors
George Pavlakos
University of Glasgow

George Pavlakos is Professor of Law and Philosophy at the School of Law, University of Glasgow. He has held visiting posts at the universities of Kiel and Luzern, the European University Institute, the UCLA Law School, the Cornell Law School and the Beihang Law School in Beijing. He is the author of *Our Knowledge of the Law* (2007) and more recently has co-edited *Agency, Negligence and Responsibility* (2021) and *Reasons and Intentions in Law and Practical Agency* (2015).

Gerald J. Postema
University of North Carolina at Chapel Hill

Gerald J. Postema is Professor Emeritus of Philosophy at the University of North Carolina at Chapel Hill. Among his publications count *Utility, Publicity, and Law: Bentham's Moral and Legal Philosophy* (2019); *On the Law of Nature, Reason, and the Common Law: Selected Jurisprudential Writings of Sir Matthew Hale* (2017); *Legal Philosophy in the Twentieth Century: The Common Law World* (2011), *Bentham and the Common Law Tradition*, 2nd edition (2019).

Kenneth M. Ehrenberg
University of Surrey

Kenneth M. Ehrenberg is Professor of Jurisprudence and Philosophy at the University of Surrey School of Law and Co-Director of the Surrey Centre for Law and Philosophy. He is the author of *The Functions of Law* (2016) and numerous articles on the nature of law, jurisprudential methodology, the relation of law to morality, practical authority, and the epistemology of evidence law.

Associate Editor
Sally Zhu
University of Sheffield

Sally Zhu is a Lecturer in Property Law at University of Sheffield. Her research is on property and private law aspects of platform and digital economies.

About the Series
This series provides an accessible overview of the philosophy of law, drawing on its varied intellectual traditions in order to showcase the interdisciplinary dimensions of jurisprudential enquiry, review the state of the art in the field, and suggest fresh research agendas for the future. Focussing on issues rather than traditions or authors, each contribution seeks to deepen our understanding of the foundations of the law, ultimately with a view to offering practical insights into some of the major challenges of our age.

Cambridge Elements≡

Philosophy of Law

Elements in the Series

Legal Personhood
Visa A. J. Kurki

The Philosophy of Legal Proof
Lewis Ross

Content-Independence in Law:Possibility and Potential
Julie Dickson

The Normativity of Law
Michael Giudice

The Nature of Authority
Kenneth Einar Himma

Legal Rights and Moral Rights
Matthew H. Kramer

Dignity and Rights
Ariel Zylberman

Contemporary Non-Positivism
Emad H. Atiq

Subsidiarity
Andreas Follesdal

The Impasse of Constitutional Rights
Jacob Weinrib

The Metaphysics of Legal Facts
Samuele Chilovi

Law's Language: Meaning and Normativity
Daniel Wodak

A full series listing is available at: www.cambridge.org/EPHL

For EU product safety concerns, contact us at Calle de José Abascal, 56–1°,
28003 Madrid, Spain or eugpsr@cambridge.org.

www.ingramcontent.com/pod-product-compliance
Lightning Source LLC
LaVergne TN
LVHW011856060526
838200LV00054B/4369